TENCHI: BUILDING A B͟~~~~~ ~~~~~~~~ ~~ HEAVEN AND E

A collection of short essays on

CW00865415

By Alister Gillies

First Edition

Published by Alister Gillies

Copyright Alister Gillies 2012

Man's Natural Heritage of Power

Contents

Foreword

I've been a martial scientist and a sincere seeker from the day I was born. The Chinese art of Kung Fu means *hard work*. You get what you give. Martial and spiritual training is no exception. Simply fixating on the technical or combative aspects of training can often miss the mark. It is the study of living wisdom in action which requires an alert awareness and correct understanding of mind and body.

Tenchi: Building a Bridge Between Heaven and Earth, is a valued addition to my extensive self-development and skill acquisition library. It effectively uses the vehicles of Zen practice and Aikido training to illustrate and guide the student on a more efficient, effortless and enjoyable path of self-discovery and mastery.

In order to benefit from this book, and apply its wisdom, you may need to review existing beliefs, values and modalities you've habitually relied upon in learning. Unlike other self-help books, that preach specific methods, *Tenchi* can help you to use the unique capacity which only you possess: the ability to truly know yourself.

I can think of no one more capable of explaining such complex practices as Zen and Aikido with humour and aplomb than Sensei Alister Gillies.

If you believe that physical and spiritual progress stems from repetitious and severe practice, Sensei Gillies will warn you of their pitfalls from personal experience. Teachers are most effective when speaking from real world experience.

Tenchi is a series of entertaining essays to walk you through the adventures of a student who's "been there". By walking in Sensei Gillies' shoes for a while, you might avoid some common pitfalls on the road.

These essays will delight and inform you, while respectfully nudging you away from the entanglements inherent in the pursuit of the exotic and esoteric.

Thong Nguyen
Founder of Kaizen Tao
Spring 2012

Preface

Searching for the Ox

Tenchi: Building a Bridge Between Heaven and Earth

Zen training and Aikido has been a source of fascination and continual learning for me over the last few decades. In the main these essays contain reflections, observations based on personal experience and opinion about the value and function of mind body training.

It is not a 'how to' book, but I have included some exercises that readers might find useful. The opinions expressed here are largely my own, except where I have quoted those of others when relevant, and do not represent the views of organisations or otherwise vested interests.

Over the time that I have been training, and I am not an expert by any means, I have seen a remarkable growth in the diversity of mind body training. As I grew into adulthood in the early to late seventies, Martial Arts training and versions of Zen training were very popular. This is less true nowadays and interest in traditional martial arts has declined, but not because those forms of training are less valuable. If anything, there is a greater variety of training techniques and forms of mind body training than ever before. There is much greater choice.

In writing these short essays I hope to provide interest and stimulation, both for those who are already interested in mind body training, and for others who might want to go on to investigate further for themselves. There is no substitute for a good teacher, and individuals who are seriously interested in taking up this kind of training should research carefully and choose accordingly.

Why should anyone choose to train and how can mind body training be of help to us? The short answer, in my opinion, is that it provides a source of power that is both natural and free. It can help us to be more fully human and alive, engage with others more productively and act as a counterbalance to the sense of isolation that is characteristic of modern life.

We live in an age marked by chronic over-consumption and rapid change. Everything is interconnected, but we seldom experience feelings of connectedness. Communications technology enables us to bridge huge distances at lightning speed, but is the quality of our communication any better?

How we consume, communicate, travel, achieve, and ultimately how we use that which nature has provided for us, has a profound impact on the quality and meaning of our lives. We are, whether we are aware of it or not, part of a huge energy exchange system; each one of us is an agent of power and has a reciprocal relationship with the whole. Cultivating that power (Jiriki [1]) is the task of mind body training.

We never fully get to understand the complete picture intellectually, but we have an innate and in-built sensibility of it as part of our human heritage – our "original face before our parents were born." It is a Zen Master's job, for example, to help wake his students up to the realisation of this 'original face' through a variety of means to a direct experience of their 'true nature'.

It is an experience that, while stretching the security of the isolated ego to the maximum, is also one that can help give birth to a more fully rounded and responsible agent of power who is at one with their own individuality, society and their environment. In different ways, and using different techniques, the task of a teacher of Aikido or Budo [2] is fundamentally no different from that of a Zen teacher – helping others to live with heart.

Food security is increasingly becoming an issue for many countries that cannot be resolved by increased production. Augmented production and massive over-consumption - particularly in developed countries - are part of the problem, not the solution. All indications from the emergent 'tiger' economies like China, India, Russia and Brazil tell us that in their headlong rush to displace the ascendency of their northern neighbours, they are replicating past errors. There is enough for man's need but not for man's greed, it would seem.

Are we really so disabled by our own desires, or just in a condition of disempowerment? As natural resources are depleted, vested interests battle to extract the last high-priced drop while the majority feel impotent and helpless. The pace of change compels us to find reserves of a different order to replace our dependence on external sources.

The future challenges us to explore who we are and the nature of power. The earth, too, tasks us to exert a more responsible stewardship. Should we fail to meet that responsibility, it may shrug us off with little more effort than a dog ridding its coat of excess water.

In some senses, the challenges of the future are no different from the challenges of the past; they are different only in scale and urgency. They are about understanding how best to use the power that is part of our heritage as human beings. For humanity this is an age old problem. First, though, we have to find and understand that power:

"If you know the enemy and know yourself, you need not fear the result of a hundred battles. If you know yourself but not the enemy, for every victory gained you will also suffer a defeat. If you know neither the enemy nor yourself, you will succumb in every battle"

Sun Tzu, *The Art of War*

Tenchi: Building a Bridge Between Heaven and Earth

Dedication

This book is dedicated in love and gratitude to my wife and to the thousands of training partners in many different parts of the world that have helped contribute to my journey.

Tenchi: Building a Bridge Between Heaven and Earth

West Meets East – The Quest for Power

Noticing the Footprints

Tenchi: Building a Bridge Between Heaven and Earth

"The farthest west is but the farthest east."

Henry Thoreau

At the beginning of the second half of the twentieth century the writing was on the wall for all to see. While the destructive force of war and the emergence of new political alliances highlighted the need for a new spirit of the age, it was to be an age marked by uncertainty.

As the new super powers surveyed their domains and the immense task of recovery ahead of them, they looked out at their powerful neighbours from behind a bristling barrage of weaponry that had the potential for mutual annihilation. Each beheld the other from an unsafe distance and an uneasy peace became the norm.

The stage was thus set for much of the last century and continues on into the present one. Walls may have come down, but we are still prisoners of our own making and increased freedom has not led to a greater sense of responsibility or security. There are new and pressing complications that come as a result of past actions. The law of cause and effect is irrevocable.

Throughout history humanity has faced similar situations. Whole civilisations have come and gone, leaving barely a trace behind. But what is different about our modern age is the intense awareness we have of our condition, fuelled by a mass media that feeds without satisfying or nourishing. We are always hungry for more it would seem. The tail truly wags the dog.

Our dilemma is that while we are highly informed about what is happening, we seem to be powerless to do anything about it. As we get smarter, we are not getting any wiser. The information super highway can be used to shape and control our choices by using the information we provide – often unwittingly - or channel destructive and harmful impulses into irrational behaviour. The use of a smart phone may galvanise a mob into action, but a mob is never smart.

More information does little to assuage the collective and individual anxiety that we experience running as an undercurrent through all of our lives. It could even be argued that it is anxiety that prompts us to buy a newspaper or switch on our information dispensers. More data and greater knowledge about the direction of travel does not appear to make the journey more satisfying.

Often we describe our problems in objective terms as something that can be managed: 'the environment', 'pollution', 'economic situation', or even the 'pace of change' itself. What we all too often fail to recognise is the source of the problem - ourselves.

Some things don't change. The 'war to end all wars' gives way to yet another 'war to end all wars'. Even the prospect of the ultimate deterrent does not really deter. Localised violence and the threat of terrorism cast a more immediate shadow that can impact on our lives without warning.

'Collateral damage' and 'acceptable risk' have become indicators of so-called manageable conflict, but the source of that conflict is seldom resolved. Unresolved personal, domestic, international and global conflicts reappear down the line to bite us on the proverbial posterior. We do not see it coming and don't listen to those that do. The many suffer at the hands of the few and we feel increasingly impotent and fatalistic.

We may have harnessed the power of the atom, but it has not left us with any more power. Perhaps we have been looking in the wrong direction, and the power that we really need is actually in front of our noses. Something is lacking, and we all know it. But where do we begin to look for the source of power?

Buddhism advocates a radical approach to power that is built upon three pillars. From an ostensibly static beginning – a seated position – one learns to regulate and develop one's breathing, posture and faculty of attention so that unity of mind and body becomes habitual. From this simple beginning one can learn the right way to live.

One gets it by 'letting go'. Letting go of what, one might ask? 'Letting go of letting go', a Zen Master may say with a humorous and annoying twinkle in his eye. Paradoxically, power comes from letting go of the desire to be powerful. This is difficult to understand, especially if you want to be powerful.

In the Aikido (a Japanese form of Budo or martial art) that Morihei Ueshiba (1883-1969) developed, the principles of mind body harmony that can be found in meditative practice are encapsulated within the kata (forms) derived from ancient Jujutsu arts. They are applied, however, in a dynamic situation as a way of training.

While it is true that the Founder of Aikido was not formally a Buddhist, he inherited a form of Shinto that was itself the result of an earlier synthesis of Buddhist theology and Shinto beliefs. There are many elements in Aikido that are common to both belief systems, particularly in relation to the insubstantial nature of the self.

The aim in Aikido is not to develop fighters, but to help develop fully rounded individuals with a more expansive sense of self who can make a productive contribution to society. In the societal realm this contributes to social and interpersonal harmony – 'wa' in Japanese.

In the personal realm, development can continue as a way of spiritual training or misogi [3] - a way of purification. How far one desires to move in this direction is a matter of individual choice and responsibility.

Within oriental culture concerns about spiritual fulfilment were traditionally left to the latter part of one's life, when one had satisfied societal and family obligations. Nowadays, however, this is less true. In Japan and throughout many western cities and towns training in Aikido is viewed as a useful way of combating the everyday stresses connected to our fast-paced, modern lifestyle.

In Europe and America, community centres and village halls host the ritualised and graceful practice of Aikido. Soft foot falls and flowing movements are punctuated by resounding and sudden thumps, as bodies are introduced to the law of gravity and the mat. In Japan salary men, women and university students typically drop into the dojo (training hall) as part of their busy daily routine, before and after work.

Aikido clearly has a therapeutic value and function, which affords a measure of training in the cultivation of mind body harmony. Indeed, there are many styles of Aikido that emphasise this aspect and understate its martial antecedents or application. Other styles, by contrast, construe themselves as thoroughly martial.

There are many in the Aikido world attracted by its philosophy of universal peace and love, and the potential for spiritual growth that the training affords. There are also just as many individuals with a more pragmatic outlook, who have little interest in the cosmology of the Founder and are more interested in Aikido's martial effectiveness.

It is an old debate, much older than Aikido. I am sure that it has been going on since the first cave dweller invented camping. But the cosmologists, taking the long view, are likely to retain the moral high ground. Their disposition is inclusive.

In between those extremes, there is a middle ground that combines elements of both, administered by the Aikikai headquarters in Tokyo. Aikido has a corporate face and the Aikikai is by far the most influential style of Aikido, with representatives in most capital cities. The organisation is headed by the Founder's grandson, Moriteru Ueshiba.

The development of modern day 'Aikikai' Aikido was the responsibility of the Founder's son, Kisshomaru Ueshiba. Morihei Ueshiba's Aikido, which continued to evolve throughout his lifetime, was a vehicle for his own personal development. He was not overly concerned with structure or organisational expansion.

The Founder had a core of senior students in different parts of Japan, with whom he visited and taught. Curiously, he taught and emphasised different things to different people, perhaps tailoring what he knew to the needs and personalities of those students. In part, this accounts for the differences in Aikido styles.

For Morihei Ueshiba the challenge facing humanity in the twentieth century was essentially spiritual, this underpinned social and economic stability. The instruction that he offered was designed to train the spirit, but the responsibility for any resulting personal transformation rested solely with the individual. The starting point in both Aikido and Zen is one's self.

The spread of Aikido and Zen Buddhism to the West in the mid 1950's, first to the US and then to Europe, was the result of a combination of social, economic and cultural factors that heralded the beginning of a new era. As nation states set about the business of post-war restoration and modernisation, it was a task framed against the backdrop of a world that was deeply divided.

Morihei Ueshiba regarded the spirit of Aiki (love and harmony) as an essential ingredient for the reunification of the Japanese people in the post-war years. He spoke of Aiki as "a golden bridge uniting the Japanese people."

In later years, after the successful introduction of Aikido to the West, he was to talk of Aiki as a "silver bridge uniting the people of the world." But it was to be some time before his vision of Aikido as a new form of 'true Budo' could be realised in his country of birth.

In Japan a heroic reconstruction was underway, fuelled by massive US investment and the need to provide a bulwark in the Pacific against Sino-Soviet interests. It was a recovery that was to bring the Japanese nation from near extinction to become a major economic super power, dominating the economy of the Pacific Basin for many years.

Immediately after the war, however, there was widespread disaffection among the Japanese population with all things connected to its militaristic past. In the eyes of the Japanese people, the leadership and values of the past were viewed with some misgivings.

This naturally included the activities and beliefs of traditional Budo and Zen Buddhism, whose ideals had been appropriated to support an ill-fated policy of Japanese nationalist expansionism. Budo was also a proscribed activity by the MacArthur led allied occupation, and it was to be some years before restrictions were relaxed.

In any event, the mass of the Japanese people were too preoccupied with day-to-day survival to be concerned about Zen or Budo. Hombu Dojo in Tokyo, the home of Aikido, served more as a hostel for the displaced and homeless in the years immediately following the war, than as a martial arts training establishment.

Many years of hardship were to follow, and it was not until the late 1950's that the hard work of the Aikido Founder's son and successor, Kisshomaru Ueshiba (1921-1999), and other committed Aikido teachers started to pay off as Aikido's popularity began to grow in Japan. In the interim, Aikido instructors had already been sent to the US and Europe by the forward thinking Japanese.

Japan now looked to the West - to the US in particular - for economic support and direction. In the West there had been considerable interest in Japanese culture prior to the war, which began to resurface when hostilities ended.

This provided Japan with an opportunity to show that the Japanese people had a gentler, more humane aspect and they were keen to share this with the world. By the early 1950s a period of cultural exchange was underway.

Japonisme was back in fashion, an echo of its seminal influence on the Impressionist, Cubist and Art Noveau movements before the war. Interest re-emerged in the wood block prints of Bertha Lum (1869-1954), an American artist who had learned carving and printing techniques from Japanese master craftsmen as early as 1907.

Lum had the distinction of being the only Western artist at the 1912 Annual Art Exhibit in Ueno Park, Tokyo. Based on the enthusiastic response to her work, Lum soon had print exhibitions at galleries in Chicago and New York. Lum's work was greatly influenced by the stories of Lafcadio Hearn, a Westerner who translated Japanese legends and fairy tales into popular books.

Much later in her life Lum was to be involved in a tragedy from which she was lucky to escape with her life, and which went largely unnoticed in the West. At the time she lived with her daughter in what is now Beijing during a period of heightened political tension. Lum was the mother-in-law of Antonio Riva, an Italian national and decorated war hero living and doing business in China.

He was unjustly arrested and put to death, allegedly for conspiring to assassinate Chairman Mao. Riva's execution and Lum's near escape, bear testimony to an era of profound world tension and the approaching deeper entrenchment of international power politics. The conflict in Korea was just around the corner.

Winter (1909), Bertha Lum

The philosophical writings of Daisetsu Teitaro Suzuki [4] (1870-1966) and Karlfried Graf Dürckheim [5] (1896-1988), helped explain many of the ideas underpinning Japanese culture and spiritual belief. Dürckheim was arrested by the Americans in Japan just after the war, where he was imprisoned for a year and a half. He later wrote:

"That time of captivity was precious to me because I could exercise zazen meditation and remain in immobility for hours."

Karlfried Graf Dürckheim

7

Translations of Haiku poetry from Japanese into English by the British academic R.H. Blyth (1898-1964), helped popularise Japanese literary forms in the early 1950s and influenced the poetic writing of a whole generation in the US and Europe.

The Italian academic, writer, photographer, ethnologist and mountaineer, Fosco Maraini (1912-2004), interned by the Japanese authorities for the last two years of the war, revisited his adopted Japanese home with obvious affection in a book published in 1955, *Meeting with Japan.*

In his book Maraini provides one of the most well informed, insightful and sympathetic accounts of Japanese life and culture to be written by a European. Italy still retains strong cultural links with Japan to this day and has a thriving Aikido community. [6]

Daisetz Tetaro Suzuki

By the mid-fifties Japanese teachers of Budo and Zen began arriving in America and Europe. And in Japan, Western students turned up on the doorsteps of Zen monasteries and martial arts' dojos. Early encounters were awkward and fumbling at first as neither side really understood the other, and imitation often took the place of understanding. But this was to change as the enthusiasm and passion of foreign students became evident to their Japanese teachers.

Japanese Aikido teachers were already instructing in Europe as early as 1951. In France, Minoru Mochizuki introduced Aikido to French Judo students, and began laying the groundwork for Tadashi Abe who was to succeed him in 1952.

In 1955, the eclectic Budo Master Kenshiro Abe took up an instructor's post at the invitation of the London Judo Society. He taught many Budo arts, including Aikido, and was to remain in Britain until 1966, when - apart from a brief visit – he returned to live permanently in Japan. In May 1959, Shunryu Suzuki (1904-1971), a Soto Zen teacher, arrived in San Francisco. Zen had come to the West to take up permanent residence.

Shunryu Suzuki

During this time Europe was also recovering from the effects of war and undergoing a period of rapid change and development. The economy of Europe began to improve, and by the mid to late 1950's, particularly in Britain, there were signs of increased prosperity – the "never had it so good" era of Harold Macmillan.

This was not just political rhetoric. The mass of the British population had never been healthier. Education, housing, health care, employment and income had all improved throughout the 1950s and into the 1960s. Slums were cleared, national service was mandatory, and people had increased leisure time and access to more financial resources than ever before.

A youth culture began to emerge in Britain for the first time. Traditional values buckled under the pressure of new and powerful social forces. Demobilised men from the services finding their way in civilian life, rebellious 'angry young men', street gangs, counter-culture groups and protest movements on both sides of the Atlantic all attested to the state of flux and uncertainty of the times.

Intellectuals rediscovered romantic naturalism and mysticism in the writings of Blake, Henry Thoreau, R.W. Emerson and Thomas Merton. The modernist poetry of Pound and Eliot, though influenced by East Asian religious thought, inspired a reaction by the poets and writers of the 'Beat Generation' against their objectivist tendencies.

Freedom and spontaneity were the watchwords of the new subjectivism of the Beat movement. 'Beat Zen' became a fashionable, though transient phenomenon in the Bohemian circles of Paris, London and New York. The literary gurus of the day included the American writers Allen Ginsberg, Jack Kerouac and William S Burroughs. For them, personal freedom came first – the 'me' generation was born.

They were a highly influential group and inspired the 'confessional' writing of Robert Lowell, Sylvia Plath, Anne Sexton and many others. But there was a self-destructive element to the movement that led some commentators to describe them as the 'Lost Generation'. Many had been inspired by the work of Wilhelm, Jung and R.H Blyth, but their connection with Eastern religion and philosophy was a tenuous one at best.

Alan Watts (1915-1973), a writer and philosopher that had connections with both the Beat Generation and the academic establishment, did a great deal to promote Eastern thought and Zen Buddhism. But, like so many of his contemporaries, the attraction of

Zen appeared to lie in the message of liberation rather than the practice.

Towards the end of his short life, however, Watts placed less emphasis on the significance of self-realisation and saw the tumultuous changes that were sweeping through society as evidence of a cosmological Zen principle – the dynamic of change itself was Zen in action. Accordingly, his interests centred on the psychology of man's alienation from nature and its effects on man's social and environmental quality of life.

The rise of secularism and the decline of religious faith, taken together with powerful forces of social change, set against the backdrop of the cold war and the omnipresent threat of a nuclear holocaust, brought everything into question. The future of mankind was itself in question.

In Paris, arguably the intellectual and cultural capital of Europe in the sixties, the existentialists gloomily pronounced that life was devoid of meaning and that the only true morality was action. A spiritual chasm opened that intellectual materialism was unable to bridge, and which traditional forms of Christian religious belief were unable to counter. Church congregations dwindled in numbers and young people began to look elsewhere for spiritual alternatives.

Many found relief in socialist inspired movements, which saw unparalleled growth during the 1950s and 60s; others looked to alternative religions and messianic prophecies promising a new age; and yet others explored alternative lifestyles and experimented with various 'mind altering' substances. The times were 'a-changin'.

Aikido and Zen proved to be especially popular in France. While the existential materialism of Sartre offered a doctrine of individual freedom through choice and action, it had a hard edged quality to it that reinforced feelings of emptiness and isolation.

Zen used similar language and talked of emptiness, freedom and action as well, but it cut off the head of the isolated self at a stroke. Self was an illusion. According to Zen Buddhism mankind is not other than nature, but part of an interconnected, dynamic whole.

It is not by accident that there are more people practicing Aikido in France today than in any other country, including Japan. The association between the French and the Japanese has always been closer than that of other occidental nations. Fosco Maraini, writing in 1955, commented on the special nature of that connection:

" I should say, in fact, that French and Japanese approach each other with the fewest mental reservations, the most open mutual humanity; that is why they achieve understanding."

Fosco Maraini

In the philosophy of Zen and Aikido, the relationship between emptiness and form represents a vibrant, creative principle in which emptiness and fullness are not mutually exclusive concepts – full is empty, and empty is full. For the Zen Buddhist being and non-being are equally illusory.

Within the extremes of existence and non-existence human beings are free to live in a spirited way that is both meaningful and rewarding. Both Zen and Aikido provide a practical, rather than an intellectual way to understand this:

e something, you already start to intellectualise it.
ntellectualise something, it is no longer what you
zuki

teachers of Budo and Zen arrived in the West they
for what they had to teach. What they had to offer,
itual training, struck a chord for those individuals
or meaning in life needed something that was both
iritual.

, way of life that addressed mankind's fundamental
ice in the inner and outer dimensions of existence.
rs came, not with definitions and philosophical
complexities, but with a heart-felt desire to spread the 'Way' (Way
of the Universe) in whatever discipline they happened to be
teaching. They taught a way of harmony.

They didn't come to replace or contest a system of belief or faith, but
to provide an antidote to the worst excesses of a rationalist world
view that had succeeded in reducing mankind to an endangered
species. They came from a country that had come perilously close to
the edge of extinction, not to teach us to fight with one another, but
how to take better care of ourselves.

Those early teachers brought part of their heritage with them from
which we could begin our own research into the nature of power and
understand our place in the universe. They came to teach us how to
build a bridge between heaven and earth.

"I want considerate people to listen to the voice of Aikido. It is not
for correcting others; it is for correcting your own mind".

Morihei Ueshiba.

Morihei Ueshiba, Founder of Aikido, 1883 1969

The Purpose of Training

Catching Sight of the Ox

"Those who are at war with others are not at peace with themselves."

William Hazlitt

Aikido is a relatively modern martial art that tacitly acknowledges links with its Koryu (Japanese Classical Budo Arts) past. It stems directly from the Daito-ryu Aikijujutsu of Sokaku Takeda (1859-1943), who departed from the Aizu clan tradition and began to teach selected individuals outside the clan system around the turn of the nineteenth century.

Sokaku Takeda

Takeda deliberately targeted dignitaries and public officials of high rank and influence as potential students, and was not averse to rejecting people of dubious character. He had a strong sense of social responsibility, and a horror of his teaching falling into the wrong hands. During his lifetime he is said to have had some thirty six thousand students. His best known student was Morihei Ueshiba, the Founder of Aikido.

Takeda himself had been taught martial skills by many different teachers, and had reformulated the techniques of Daito-ryu that had originally been taught to him by his father and the priest Ginshin Hoshina. The origins of Daito-ryu are far from clear, but it is believed that the art has the same root as Sumo in an ancient art called Tegoi.

The art of Tegoi, it is claimed, was passed down from the descendants of the Emperor Seiwa (858-876), through the Seiwa-Genji family line. Shinra Saburo Minamoto no (Genji) Yoshimitsu (1045–1127) was instrumental in much of its later modifications, adapting the art as circumstances and knowledge permitted.

Yoshimitsu is said to have been responsible for the formal codifying of the 'secret' Aiki techniques that make both Daito-ryu and Aikido so distinctive. It is also known that Yoshimitsu studied Chinese military tactics, and it is at least likely that there are other Chinese influences in the art's formation.

In actual fact very little is known about the obscure art of Tegoi, and only oblique references can be found in the Shinto text 'Kojiki' (Records of Ancient Matters). According to Tokimune Takeda (1916-1993), the late Headmaster of Daito-ryu, it was Sumo and its core "Aiki In-Yo (yin-yang) method" that constituted the basic techniques of Daito-ryu Aiki Jujutsu.

Masanori Hoshina (1611-1673) was an important figure in the subsequent development of Daito-ryu in the seventeenth century, revising the art into a self-defence art called Oshikiuchi (lit., court self-defence art). He also studied the secret sword arts of Onoha Itto Ryu. The transmission of these two arts, Onoha Itto Ryu and Oshikiuchi, became a mandatory requirement for the retainers of succeeding Aizu Lords.

Oshikiuchi was taught in the main to nobility - both male and female - and contained large movements with wide stances (for use when wearing armour), and smaller range movements for instances when movement was cramped (in residential areas, and during formal occasions).

As the term 'uchi' (inside) would suggest, it was an art that was confined to the inner circle of the court. At a time of conflict, when all outer defences had been overcome, the last battle would be staged in the restricted confines of the court where large movements were impracticable.

When Morihei Ueshiba reworked Takeda's basic techniques in his formulation of Aikido, he was doing no less than Yoshimitsu, Hoshina and Takeda had done before him. Aiki is a mind body quality implicit in the execution of technique, rather than a series of prescribed physical movements. It permits infinite variety and interpretation in the way that the principles of yin and yang (in and yo) are utilised.

Examples of Aiki movement can be seen in the current techniques of Daito-ryu and Aikido. It is exemplified in the present day students of Yukiyoshi Sagawa (1902-1998) and Kodo Horikawa (1894-1980), former students of Sokaku Takeda. However, exactly how Aiki was transmitted by teachers in the past has always been shrouded in mystery, and either deliberately not explained or reserved for students admitted to the inner (uchi) circle.

Both Horikawa and Sagawa contributed their own unique expression to the arts taught by Takeda, and their successors continue to do the same. A teaching license issued by Kodo Horikawa, explicitly granted one of his students, Seigo Okamoto, the right to create his own techniques.

Aiki is an essentially creative principle that permits and informs the mastery of basic technique. Without Aiki, technique would be little more than choreographed movement. Sokaku Takeda was regarded as an unrivalled master of his day, and his influence and mastery has contributed greatly to the development of Aiki arts.

In one sense he was a relic of an age past, inculcating conservative values and principles that looked backwards in time. In another important sense, he was a guardian of knowledge and skills that were in danger of being lost as Japan made the transition from its feudal past to the modern age.

What he taught contained the seeds of an ethical and moral system that embodied Confucian notions of self-control, social harmony, etiquette, respect for elders and obedience to the teacher - ideals that are still very much alive in modern day Japan. While there was undoubtedly an element of personal development in the study of Daito-ryu Aikijujutsu, it remained understated under Takeda's direction.

The importance of the individual in Japan has always been subordinate to that of the group or society. This is reflected in the primacy of values that reinforce conformity within the framework of a vertically structured, hierarchical system. 'Wa', or social harmony, is everything in Japan.

Morihei Ueshiba's teaching differed from Takeda's in the unprecedented emphasis that he placed on Aikido as a vehicle for personal transformation. In this respect, Ueshiba was influenced as much by his connection with the charismatic Onisaburo Deguchi (1871-1948) and the Omoto Kyo religion, as by his own spiritual insights.

While Takeda was more concerned with passing on effective techniques for actual combat for the restoration and preservation of social order and harmony, Ueshiba's focus was explicitly on harmony in the heart of the individual. For Ueshiba, inner harmony underpinned social concord.

The tensions between Takeda and Ueshiba were not only those of a protégé and mentor, or an individualist versus a collectivist orientation, they were the result of a fundamental difference in their understanding of the nature of Budo itself.

Ueshiba's approach was radically different: Aikido was a Budo of love and the 'divine techniques' of the art were 'misogi', a way of spiritual purification. His Budo was for the modern age; the age of steel and blood had gone.

The Founder of Aikido dedicated his entire life to finding a way of bridging heaven and earth, using Budo as a vehicle. His martial studies, intuition, religious experience and knowledge of the Chinese and Japanese classics all informed him that such unification was possible.

But when Morihei Ueshiba split from Sokaku Takeda, he also carried with him the seeds of a martial/spiritual dichotomy that took him many years to resolve. That he was successful in unifying these opposing elements in his own life and practice singles him out as a unique individual in the history of the martial arts.

When he died he left behind the legacy of a path that he had pioneered personally, but this did not necessarily make it any easier for those who came after. A teacher may point the way, but only the student can travel its length. To this day there is still some tension between the martial and spiritual aspects of Aikido, with some styles claiming that they are more 'realistic' (martial), and others that they are more 'spiritual'.

Morihei Ueshiba may have left behind a system of teaching and practice that contains at its core the opportunity to resolve the apparently irreconcilable, but it is not a method that guarantees it. Each student, regardless of style or affiliation, must find their own way to the heart of what Aikido offers.

Unlike many other modern martial arts in Japan, Aikido is not sports oriented. Although there is a style of Aikido that was developed by one of the Founder's early students (Tomiki), that was specifically adapted with competition in mind, it has not proved as popular as might have been expected. Aikido remains non-competitive in its essential nature and current practice.

In most respects Aikido is very typically Japanese. In this sense it very closely resembles what is collectively referred to as Haragei in Japan, the cultivation and development of Hara (the seat of spiritual power in the abdomen) in a chosen activity. It is in this regard that Aikido, Zen and many other arts can be said to converge, or at the very least, be seen as having a common root or cultural flavour.

If Aikido is construed as Haragei, then it is possible to locate it firmly within a broad cultural tradition that encapsulates both modern martial arts, Koryu arts, Zen training and many other art forms that have no direct martial application. In Japan, such arts have traditionally been the mainstay for the transmission of social behaviour and morals designed to support individual development and social cohesion.

The martial arts of Japan are not simply techniques for life and death situations of conflict; they are also a way of mind, body and spirit cultivation for the whole person and society at large. They exemplify the concrete expression of philosophical and moral values drawn from Confucianism, Taoism, Buddhism and Shinto.

The test of whether something is Haragei or not is determined, amongst other things, by its longevity – does it stand the test of time? Does it function as a way of enriching one's life in the present; is it meaningful and rewarding in itself; and does it extend beyond itself and filter into one's daily life and society at large?

In his book *Hara: The Vital Centre of Man*, philosopher and Zen practitioner Karlfried Graf Dürckheim writes that when Haragei is cultivated:

"An all-around transformation of all one's faculties takes place, unhindered by the limitations of the five senses and the intellect. One perceives reality more sensitively, is able to take in perceptions in a different way, assimilates them and therefore reacts differently and, finally radiates something different...The three fundamental reactions to life and the world—perception, assimilation, and response—change in the direction of an expansion, deepening, and intensifying of the whole personality."

Durkheim's book describes Haragei as a quality of presence in which the sensibility of the belly is fully integrated into any activity, from the subtle ritual of the traditional tea ceremony to the focused intent of an archer drawing their bow, or the graceful stroke of a calligrapher's brush. It is present in Aikido when the art is cultivated to its optimum level.

Within this tradition of Haragei, the emphasis has always been on what D.T. Suzuki, the Zen Buddhist scholar, described as radical empiricism - finding out for one's self. From this point of view, it is not surprising that the Founder of Aikido (and other Japanese teachers since his time) did not explain what they were teaching beyond the necessary forms of kata (prescribed forms).

Some Japanese teachers even assert that they will take what they know with them when they die. This is incomprehensible to the average Westerner, and perhaps some modern day Japanese, too. But it is perfectly in line with a mode of teaching in which the student bears most of the weight of the learning process. Haragei is not something a teacher can give to a student.

If one accepts that Aikido has a history, which it undoubtedly has, then it is clear that Morihei Ueshiba underwent an apprenticeship, drawing his martial skills from a variety of sources and teachers within the world of classical Budo. From the view point of Haragei, the individual details or technical sources of his skills are not particularly relevant unless they can shed light on what is ultimately a transformative experience. A skilled teacher can help with learning form, but the student must do the main part to develop sufficient awareness and sensitivity.

There are many Haragei arts in Japan, and although the external forms differ from art to art, there are 'internal' features that are common to all. Most Japanese understand this and refer to the martial arts using the generic description 'belly arts'.

In Aikido, for example, many of the Founder's students went on to develop their own style of Aikido that, while sharing the common name Aikido, became quite distinct from one another. But from the perspective of Haragei it all makes sense – it enfolds diversity within its perspective without contradiction:

"Equality without discrimination is poor equality; discrimination without equality is poor discrimination" - Chinese mirror verse.

The path of Haragei, shared by Aikido and many other arts, is broad with a long tradition and history. It is contained in the Soto Zen tradition of Dogen that came from China and flowered in Japan. It is deeply interwoven into the fabric of the culture and psyche of the Japanese people.

'One Point', 'Seika Tanden' and 'Centre' are terms commonly found in Aikido, but these terms do not fully convey the significance of Hara. They are starting points at the beginning level from which the student can progress – as Dürckheim explains, to experience the "ground of being" and its connection to the "totality of being" in activities of everyday life.

The Founder of Aikido alludes to such an experience in this verse, framed in his own idiosyncratic style:

"Create each day anew by clothing yourself with heaven and earth, bathing yourself with wisdom and love, and placing yourself in the heart of Mother Nature."

At the heart of Japanese Budo and Zen is the fundamental belief that the realisation of our 'true nature' is man's natural heritage. Tomio Otani, one of the original pioneers of Japanese Budo in Britain, wrote in the early 1960s of the purpose of Budo:

"The highest purpose of Budo is to awaken mankind's spirit to the direct realisation of our true nature."

Beginnings

Getting Hold of the Ox

Tenchi: Building a Bridge Between Heaven and Earth

"I have scarcely touched the sky and I am made of it."

Antonio Porchia

I first started practicing Aikido while a student at the University of Glasgow in 1982. I had no previous experience of martial arts, but this was to be the start of a lifelong study and fascination with what is one of the most subtle and refined arts to have come from the islands of Japan. Thirty years later, I feel that I have barely scratched the surface. For me, it is an enduring study that begins anew each day. It begins from where I am standing.

Aikido is not simply a non-dualistic philosophy, but a practical system of mind body cultivation through the medium of body arts that have their origin in Japan's feudal past. There is some evidence that its origins are even older. Some say that it can be traced back to the time of Bodhidarma and his arrival in China (502-557 A.D.).

My interest in mind body matters predates beginning Aikido and goes back to an earlier time in my life. As an adolescent I was troubled by chronic stomach pains. At school I was unable to come to terms with my total inability to learn mathematics. I worried about this incessantly, and soon developed a neurotic frame of mind that dreaded the prospect of each and every maths lesson.

Teachers were not at all sympathetic, and seemed to believe that I was being deliberately stupid. This was not true, of course, but the experience did help to sow the seeds of self-doubt and undermine whatever confidence I had. Adolescence can be a delicate time.

It wasn't until many years later that I understood that I suffered from chronically low self-esteem, itself the by-product of a dysfunctional family background and exacerbated by the constant relocations enforced by my father's occupation in the military.

Moving from place to place and from school to school involved a constant game of catch up. As a consequence, I was to see-saw between the extremes of arrogant rebelliousness and withdrawal for quite a few years, and had a protracted and unnaturally long adolescence that continued into my mid-twenties and beyond.

At the age of 15, while algebra, calculus, trigonometry, geometry and most of the sciences sailed over my head, I read anything and everything connected with the gothic, the macabre, the esoteric and what is now termed mind body. I was just as at ease reading Edgar Allan Poe and the texts from the Upanishads.

One experience involving meditation, that was to be repeated many years later, stands out for me as unique and remarkable from this time. After yet another sleepless night enduring the tortuous burning in my stomach that had being going on for months, I had had enough. I could not endure the long, agonising nights covered in cold sweat and that insistent acid irritation any longer. I resolved that I was going to do something about it.

Doctors could find nothing wrong with me and had ascribed the symptoms to 'growing pains', but I did not believe them (later in my early twenties an endoscope discovered scar tissue in my duodenum, evidence of a duodenal ulcer that had healed).

I had been reading a book on yoga and meditation. In this book there were various claims about mind over matter that had made a strong impression on my adolescent mind. I decided that I would follow the instructions on meditation to see if I could somehow overcome my chronic stomach pains. I felt naively sure that this would work, or rather I was determined that it would and was prepared, somewhat wilfully, to go to any extremes.

I had no understanding of what meditation involved. I simply followed the instructions: crossed my legs, made my spine straight, and concentrated my attention on my breath, focussing on nothing but the breathing.

I soon learned that it wasn't so easy. Suddenly there were thousands of reasons to do something else. I experienced a profound sense of unease, and fought against the urge to twitch and squirm. It was difficult just to sit still. The pain in my legs and back became excruciating, but I was determined to follow it through or die in the attempt.

I remember being racked with pain from every possible source in my body, including my stomach, and having to fight against the urge to get up. It was as if every fibre in my body wanted to do anything but sit in that position. I continued. The discomfort seemed to go on forever, and sweat streamed down my face and body from the effort.

I had no idea where all this was going, but I was absolutely determined to see it through to whatever end it would come to – even my own. I concentrated with all my might, forcing myself to ignore the pain.

Then all of a sudden I found myself coming back into conscious awareness. I wondered what had happened. Where had I been? Had I blacked out? How much time had passed? These thoughts arose in a very calm matter of fact way. They were somehow detached, as if they were not my own - not even very important. They appeared to be coming out of some silent and calm space that was both very alien, yet perfectly normal at the same time. It was a strange but pleasant feeling.

I mentally checked my posture to see if my body had slumped – surely I had been unconscious? But no, my legs were crossed and my back was still straight. My head hadn't even fallen forward, as it would if I had fallen asleep. What had happened?

Then my awareness shifted to focus quietly on this question. A bright light suddenly switched on inside my head. It got brighter and brighter and felt like it was not going to stop. I became frightened and opened my eyes. It stopped.

I managed to disentangle my legs, which had gone numb, and when the circulation returned went downstairs. The house was unnaturally silent. There was a powerful smell of cleaning fluids that I had never noticed before.

My senses felt unusually acute. The house was so quiet that I had the impression that there must have been some sort of accident outside. I even opened the front door, half expecting to see a hushed crowd gathered around some unfortunate victim of an explosion or car crash. Everything was normal - but not quite the same.

Many years later I realised that it was the quietude and calmness of my mind that made things seem this way. What I had experienced was a profound inner stillness of mind. As a child I had no frame of reference to understand this and had attributed an inner condition to some external event.

The stomach pains had gone, but they came back a few weeks later and continued intermittently until my mid to late twenties. I tried to meditate, but couldn't concentrate or sit for very long. I gave it up and thought little about the experience as I passed into adult life. But the memory has always remained with me. I did not share it with family members or friends, and did not understand what had happened until over two decades had passed.

When I left school I joined the Merchant Navy, seduced by exotic stories of foreign lands, colourful descriptions (tall tales) and sunny climates. I travelled extensively throughout the Far East and thoroughly enjoyed the experience. At that time I had no interest in martial arts, although I had been to Japan and had 'called in' to Tokyo, Kobe, Yokohama, and Osaka several times.

On one trip I came across a book in the ship's library by Christmas Humphreys, entitled Zen Buddhism. I put it away, but did not read it until several months later when I was at home on leave. I read it in one sitting, and it made perfect sense. I remember laughing out loud as I finished reading the book - and the puzzled glances from my parents. It all made sense, until I began thinking about it. I learned that Zen Buddhism requires practice.

One of the consequences of living an itinerant lifestyle is a feeling of being unsettled in life; while travel can be liberating and rewarding in many ways, it can also be very limiting. As friends and colleagues settled down in life, I began to feel more and more isolated. Life seemed meaningless and I had no sense of direction. I began to search for meaning.

Many people define themselves, in the most superficial sense, by geographical location or nationality - everyone has to come from, or belong to, somewhere. Home is where it all begins.

There is a whole mythology built around the concept of home as an idealised entity. There's no place like it, we are reminded.

But there are many different kinds of home. Psychotherapists inform us that we are conditioned by our family of origin, and that the quality and character of our inner or psychological life is determined by our earliest experiences. Since there have never been any perfect parents, it follows that there are no perfect children.

Freedom, in psychological terms, is freedom from the tyranny of negative past experiences that continue to exert harmful pressures in the present. We are not to blame for our current unhappiness, but we are responsible for doing something about it.

Neither are our parents responsible, and we cannot fairly hold them to account, except in the most extreme cases of criminal abuse and cruelty. They too have acted from past and unseen influences of which they were largely unconscious.

The past has gone and only the present remains; this is where the work of self-awareness begins. How we define ourselves in the present can be the gateway to psychological and spiritual health, or to lifelong suffering and unhappiness.

But standing guard at that gateway is fear. We are afraid to look too closely at ourselves because we are afraid of what we might or might not find. Fear of self has long been acknowledged by psychoanalysis as the limiting factor in therapeutic interventions. Patients will only go so far.

Carl Jung, one of the Founders of the psychoanalytic movement, noted that when treating his patients some of them - those he did not expect to recover - underwent a sudden and transformative experience and became well. This caused Jung to believe that the process of psychoanalysis served as a sort of catalyst in some instances, triggering a transformational process that he could not fully understand. He further believed that if this process was to be understood, it would revolutionise psychology.

In the East this transformational process has been understood for thousands of years, and training in the mind body connection provides the catalyst through which healing and self-realisation can occur. Training in Zen is sometimes referred to as the way of the 'gateless gate'. But it is not a gate to be entered lightly, or indeed one that guarantees freedom from life's ills.

Although Jung understood the significance of the mind body relation, he did not believe that Eastern mysticism was suitable for the Western mind, mainly because of the fundamental cultural differences in what he called archetypes, those innate ideas and symbols that lie deep in the unconscious. However, towards the later part of his life Jung began to shed some of his earlier ambivalence towards Eastern ideas. His fascination with the Chinese *Yi Jing*

(*Book of Changes* 1122 B.C.) led directly to his work on *Synchronicity*.

Japanese Buddhism has many different sects. Some, like Zen Buddhism, focus on the cultivation of Jiriki, or self-power, as a means of attaining realisation of Buddha Nature. Others, most notably the Pure Land School, emphasise Tariki, or other power, a principle of unconditional love and compassion as the very foundation of life. But they are not separate; the difference is merely one of emphasis.

Jiriki is the preparation for Tariki. Some sects go even further and say that there is no such thing as Jiriki, "all is Tariki." The difference can perhaps be best illustrated by the idea of 'Buddha Turning Away' and 'Buddha Turning Towards'.

In the former case, the Buddha in turning away is leading the way by example. If we follow his ascetic practices we will eventually come to realisation. In the second case, it is assumed that we are already living in the right way and realisation (Buddha) will come to us naturally. The important point, which applies in both cases, is not to deliberately look for enlightenment.

Zen masters are not interested in how we define ourselves. They don't care about who we think we are, or whether we have an inferiority or superiority complex. If one's ego has got one to the Zendo, then that's fine. The rest is unimportant.

The master will be seen at dokusan (formal interview), and a Koan (public case, or riddle) will be assigned to each student individually. This Koan will point directly at Buddha nature. Each student will have to find their own way, if they can. A typical koan could be:

"Two hands clap and there is a sound. What is the sound of one hand?"

For me Buddhism was a good fit. It appeared to be the most rational and psychological of religions, and it offered a way of being settled from the inside out. Being unsettled from an early age, and conditioned by circumstances to a rootless sort of life, it felt right that I should learn to be more at home with myself. I already knew that I was my own worst enemy, and the discipline would do me some good.

As a young adult I began to practice Zazen in an erratic self-taught fashion that in time became more established with regular sitting practice. I even attended a few retreats. My health improved and in my mid-thirties I had another experience very similar to the first one at fifteen.

Like before, I experienced coming back into conscious awareness together with the same intense sense of inner illumination. As on the previous occasion, when I opened my eyes it stopped. This time, however, as I looked around at the familiar surroundings of my room I felt that my relationship to everything was different.

It was as if I was looking at everything with the eyes of a new born child. All the familiar objects around me seemed vital and fresh with their own unique quality. I remember laughing a lot, and at times crying. This lasted for about three days.

I continued with sitting meditation, and tried to recapture the experience in my practice, but the more I chased it the more elusive it proved to be. I still didn't really understand what had happened, but I had read some accounts of 'kensho' and 'awakening' experiences and understood that I had gone through a similar, but perhaps milder form of what was described in the literature. But I could not be sure.

One thing I did understand, however, was that there was an element of fearfulness that was somehow holding me back. I felt stuck, and although I continued to practice, this sense of 'stuckness' was always in the background.

There was a lot I did not understand, and as my practice was mainly an isolated one – I did not belong to any group or organisation – I felt sure that other, more experienced practitioners would be able to help. I decided to attend a retreat.

In some ways I was at a crossroads. I had already started practicing Aikido and had developed a passionate interest in the art, and while each form of training satisfied different needs, those needs had begun to pull me in different directions.

While I found deep relaxation and calmness in Zazen, I could not find the same qualities at that time in Aikido – that was to come much later.

Both Zen training and Aikido training requires considerable commitment in order to make any real progress, but the nature of that commitment is different. Aikido is a social activity and one practices with others.

In Zen one is on one's own; dependence on others is not encouraged. Students are directed to find the 'teacher within' from the beginning. With a few exceptions, trainees are discouraged in forming an attachment to a particular master or teacher.

Aikido training takes place 'in the world', whereas serious Zen training occurs in a more cloistered and regulated monastic environment where distractions are minimal. At least that is how it seemed to me at the time.

But that was to change. Partly as a result of Zen training itself, and partly as a result of the nature of my commitment to that training, my perspective on Zen changed quite dramatically. I also found that it was possible to adapt one's training as circumstances changed, but that came later. I was to learn that I did not have to choose between Aikido and Zen; in both cases I had a long way to go.

While there are some similarities between Aikido and Zen, there are also some significant differences. Aikido is often described as 'moving Zen', but this is a superficial and somewhat figurative expression that conveys very little and does neither any real justice. It would be just as pointless, for example, to describe Zen as 'static Aikido'.

It seems to me now that while Zen is not Aikido, and Aikido is certainly not Zen, I am able to understand them both a little more. The 'not' of something can be very illuminating. But it is true to say that my interest in Aikido came from Zen training, at least originally.

When I first saw Aikido being practiced I felt an immediate affinity with the art. Some part of me could comprehend what was happening on the mat with ease. But it was many years before I could reproduce anything like the graceful and powerful movements that first captivated my attention. Aikido is simple, but people can be complicated. I was no exception.

At a retreat hosted by a Buddhist Soto order in the North East of England, I came to a realisation that completely changed my outlook forever. On the day before the end of the seven day retreat, the Guest Master of the Monastery came to me and asked if I would be going or staying, now that the end of the week was near. I replied that I didn't know, but I would decide on the following day.

I had found the training demanding, but had experienced no startling revelations. Other than constant tiredness – that mysteriously disappeared at bed time – and some mild hallucinations during meditation practice, nothing remarkable had occurred.

Sitting in formal meditation for six hours every day, mindfulness practice while walking (Kinhin), working, eating and during social occasions, had been a challenging experience for me. This was my first long retreat and I didn't know what to make of it, but I was staying for the final day and would see it through to the end.

During the morning service on the last day, as I became absorbed in the resonant chanting of the monks' as they intoned the names of all the patriarchs through the ages, I had a sudden and powerful insight into the depth and nature of their lives. It came as a shock, wholly unexpected and without any conscious intent on my part.

I suddenly understood, with a feeling of total clarity, that the ordered lives of these monks with their rituals and ascetic discipline sprang from a deep well of compassion for human suffering. I could almost taste it. Of course I had thought that I knew this before arriving at the retreat, but the reality was entirely different. I now understood it with my whole being; my previous understanding seemed glib and superficial by comparison.

I found the experience completely overwhelming, and it triggered a corresponding feeling of compassion for my own condition within myself, as a kind of aftershock. I understood that I did not have to do this – there was absolutely no need to force myself to engage in severe ascetic practice.

I realised that my Zen practice had been founded on negative self-judgement. I had believed that it would in some way make me a better person. Now I knew that fundamentally there was nothing that could be made better or worse. As a result, my practice was to change completely.

I had been practicing a kind of macho-spirituality for years, and now there was no longer any reason for me to be so hard on myself. I felt an immense burden from my unsettled childhood that had overshadowed much of my adult life lifting; more importantly, I could feel what had been obscured. I grieved for the nature that had been forced to retreat behind a fearful, angry and reserved protective shell.

Tears of compassion, relief and gratitude flowed together at the same time, and I knew with an unshakable certainty that I was going back home to my ordinary life. As powerful as this experience was, it was just the beginning of a different, more relaxed level of Zen training.

Buddhist monks take a vow to save all sentient beings. It is not a vow that is taken lightly. They understand the nature of delusion and as a result do not judge the condition of others. Through training they learn to open their hearts to compassion, which allows a glimpse of the true self nature that is veiled by illusory consciousness. With consistent practice this compassion naturally extends to all sentient beings.

While I understood and appreciated the monks' commitment and purpose, the selfless nature and value of their activity, I realised that I was only at the beginning. In many ways my time at the retreat had been cathartic, and I felt that the austerities of monastic life were not for me at that time.

When I left, I left with feelings of respect and admiration, humbled and grateful for the experience. I also left feeling lighter and with a fresh sense of perspective for the road ahead.

Whenever I think of those men and women, and of the monastery built with their own hands on that wild and exposed moor land hill in the North East of England, I see them as a kind of remote power station. Whatever the weather, regardless of what is happening in the wider world, they are there quietly generating power. They are generating and extending love and compassion for all people. Sometimes I imagine I can hear them.

My short stay at the monastery had given me a little glimpse of Zen. But it was only later in the days and weeks that followed that I really appreciated the depth and value of the training. For two to three weeks afterwards, each day was spent in pleasant tranquillity, each waking moment a pleasure and each night a restful, deep sleep. Someday I would like to go back.

The monks at the monastery had hinted that I had had a 'kensho' like experience, but they did not regard it as anything out of the ordinary. On reflection, I am sure that they did not want to encourage any undue conceit on my part, or unwarranted degree of attachment to what is still, in the great scheme of things, a transitory phenomenon. In Zen, the point of arrival is also the point of departure.

For the next few years Zen training faded into the background, not entirely neglected, but certainly not as prominent as it had been. Aikido was my main passion. The movement of Aikido, both graceful and powerful with its spiralling and circular motions, had me enthralled.

In Aikido opposition is neutralised not by defeating the attacker with a decisive blow, but by the attacker's intent being assimilated into the vital centre of a technique to join with the centre of the defender. Both centres then move as one.

If the initial intent of the attacker is inharmonious, as attacks usually are, this will be reflected in the posture and centre of the attacker. When such intent comes into play with another centre that is calm, relaxed and 'connected' to the Universe (in harmony), the resultant centrifugal or centripetal movement of the technique will be overwhelming to the attacker.

Finding that centre within one's self, learning to connect with the centre of others, and ultimately forgetting centre entirely as it becomes totally integrated into one's life, is no small task. For most people this takes a life time to accomplish, even under the guidance of an experienced teacher.

Aikido takes considerable practice. When performed at an optimal level Aikido seems effortless, belying the amount of effort and time that goes into making it look so easy. It is not by accident that the most accomplished practitioners are in their seventies and upwards.

Those that are the most advanced, however, seldom see themselves in this way. The Founder of Aikido, Morihei Ueshiba, vehemently protested against suggestions that he should train less arduously, claiming when he was eighty three, *"I am still in the midst of my training."*

I had come to Zen training looking for a kind of 'fix-it-all', a solution to all my existential quandaries, so it should not be surprising that I had similar expectations from Aikido. In time, of course, these fell away. What was left behind was the practice.

But it came to be a practice of expression, rather than a quest for some 'other-worldly' experience, insight or enlightenment. Through Aikido I learned to work with 'connection' or 'centre', referred to as 'sei-chu-sen' (heart mind), a vertical axis through the centre of the body. Nowadays I find this practice rewarding in and of its self.

There was a time when I craved enlightenment. There was a time when I wanted to be better at Aikido, to be better than others in this non-competitive art. I was to realise that what we practice is what we get good at. So I got good at being ambitious and my craving for enlightenment got stronger. In terms of Buddhist iconography, I was 'feeding the hungry ghosts'. The more we feed them the hungrier they get. I learned to stop feeding them.

In Native American culture there is a folk story about a grandfather and grandchild. The child asks the grandfather why is there so much confusion and suffering in the world. The grandfather replies that in the heart of every human being there are two dogs. One dog is very contented, loving and obedient. The other is always angry, selfish and greedy. Sometimes they fight with each other. When the child asked which dog usually won, the grandfather replied: "the one you feed the most."

In current times people can become obsessed by grading and rank. In the world of the martial arts this is a relatively recent phenomenon, and comes from what in Japan is called the 'Gendai' period, following the Meiji restoration (1868) in which Japan was engaged in rapid Westernisation. Prior to this time, during what is known as the Koryu phase, ranking in the martial arts was not so formal.

A white belt became a black belt through time and use, the result of natural discolouration and wear and tear. In the fullness of time, it would return to white through the same process. Whether in Zen training or Aikido, having a beginners mind is indispensable to progress. This is called 'shoshin' in Japanese (sometimes termed 'nyuanshin' – soft or flexible mind). In my own case, it has taken me quite some time to learn to be a beginner. I am still learning.

"In the beginner's mind there are many possibilities, in the expert's mind there are few."

(Shunryu Suzuki, *Zen Mind Beginner's Mind*)

Being Present and Letting Go

Taming the Ox

"You can only lose what you cling to."

Buddha

For a long time I was the proverbial 'Zen Goose' in a bottle. The harder I tried to crack the outer casing to set the goose free, the more impenetrable it seemed. Severity was not the answer.

Sometimes there was an audible 'pop' as liberation appeared close, but it was only the gooses' head protruding through the neck of the bottle. Yes, the air was fresher, but I was still stuck, unable to pull my goose rump up from below.

Many people knock at the doors of monasteries and dojos. They all want the same thing, in one way or another. They all want to be happy.

Happiness, according to the Dalai Lama, *"is our natural heritage as human beings."* So too is enlightenment. It is our natural condition, our 'true nature'. But it doesn't come easily. For most of us, it requires work.

The more we try to grasp hold of it, the more elusive it becomes. Karlfried Graf Dürckheim rightly identifies the Western difficulty with Eastern thought as "trying to make an internal into an external." Thankfully there is a remedy. It exists in the present right in front of our noses.

Buddhism tells us that everything is potentially a dharma vehicle – a source of teaching. Some vehicles are designated as greater than others, but they are vehicles just the same. A ferry, for example, is a means of conveying a traveller from one side of the river to the other. When the other side is reached, it doesn't make any sense to carry the ferry throughout the rest of the journey. But this is precisely what the mass of people do. Human beings become attached.

But aren't attachments necessary and unavoidable? We can't all retreat into the forest and live in a blissful state of nirvana. What's wrong with attachment? We might argue that it's not possible to live without love, affection, relationships and a whole gamut of needs and desires. Doesn't their satisfaction provide the motivation to live a fulfilling and happy life?

The reason for suffering, according to the Buddha, is attachment. At the root of attachment is desire. What do we desire? We desire the end of suffering. We are like a dog chasing its own tail.

Often we are so caught up in our own struggle to be free that the more we struggle the more ensnared we become. So what are we to do? We can let go. How do we let go? We find a practice that will help us unite heaven and earth. Uniting heaven and earth is a process of letting go. Life is letting go, *"until there is not a trace left"*, as one Zen master said. It is happening anyway, so why not get with the programme?

In Zen they refer to a condition known as 'mind body fallen away', or 'mind body dropped off'. At one time I imagined that this was some sort of mystical experience of 'oneness' with the universe, in which one's individuation becomes suspended, or integrated into the larger cosmos. It was so far away and unattainable that naturally I desired it.

Looking back, my fanciful ideas about mind body might seem a bit foolish and immature, but on reflection I now see it as a very useful projection. My fantasy, delusion, or 'mind-weed', as the late Suzuki Roshi may have called it, was not wasted. It kept me sitting in meditation for quite some time. It fed my practice. During countless hours of silent meditation something took root and began to grow. I was not aware of it at the time, but my practice was ripening.

The condition of 'mind body fallen away' refers to a state of mind body unification, in which mind and body are connected through the 'tanden', an area roughly two inches below the navel. When concentrating one's mind in this location, the body relaxes and one's centre of gravity naturally begins to settle in the lower abdomen.

With time a feeling of wholeness and emotional stability becomes established. The tanden is simply a focal point. In reality there is no such physiological place, and although one may experience a sensation of warmth in this area during meditation, this is due to increased blood flow in the abdominal area.

The relationship between mind and body in Zen resembles the way in which the sympathetic and parasympathetic nervous systems function as part of the autonomic nervous system. If we take the autonomic system as an analogous self, and its two components as representing mind and body, then we have some idea of how it works.

From a neurological perspective, the relationship between calmness and excitement is mirrored in the way we react to emotional stimuli. When we become angry, shocked, or afraid for example, the sympathetic nervous system is in a state of high activity. When we are relaxed, happy, or asleep, then the parasympathetic system predominates.

Each acts as a check upon the other maintaining a healthy degree of equilibrium. In Zen the relationship between mind and body is one of 'steady state' equilibrium. In Zen parlance it is 'of its self so'.

Just as the eyes do not see themselves seeing, or the tongue taste itself tasting, in mind body fallen away the mind body does not see itself, as it were, 'mind-bodying'. It is a condition of profound calmness. It comes of itself as a result of practice.

In Aikido, mind body unification provides the basis for a very stable and powerful centre wherein the practitioner has access to the whole of the body, rather than isolated muscle groups. In turn, with repeated practice and experience, this gives rise to a particular relaxed subjective feeling or 'energy body' that is called Ki (Chi in Chinese). Initially, this has a somewhat self-conscious quality to it, but gives way to a more natural feeling with appropriate training - a bit like driving a car.

In Eastern thought man is seen as a universe in miniature. By creating a pathway from the crown of the head down to the perineum, where vital energy can accumulate and circulate, man is able to unify heaven and earth (mind body).

In Zen this energy is called Jiriki (spiritual power or concentrative energy), and it is through the accumulation of this energy by means of regular sitting that mind body unification occurs. Letting go, I was to learn, was about letting go of duality. But that was only the beginning.

Not all people find what they are looking for. Some find something else; some don't really know what they want at all, and others take what they can get. Yet others cling to what they find, fearful that it should be taken from them. Few understand that if you let it go, whatever you have found can come back to you. If it does not come back, it doesn't really matter – it was not yours in the first place.

Each moment in life is a gift that passes, never to return. If you stay in the present it is possible to be open to what each moment affords. This is non-attachment. Time, like food well chewed, does more for you when it is taken slowly. To take full advantage of time, however, requires a present frame of mind.

But how present are we? In all ages mankind has exhibited an appealing vulnerability. Through this intrinsic neediness we are compelled to associate with others and take up membership of a community. Our salvation lies in that innate neediness. Mankind in normal circumstances cannot live alone. Our condition is one of dependence, and it is this dependent origination that gives rise to what Buddhists term the 'entanglements of the senses'.

Buddhism is a doctrine that offers liberation from the entangled self. Being fully present with an entangled self is not easy, however. The entangled self is by nature resistant. It resides deep in the subconscious like a three year old in a supermarket, unpredictable and difficult to manage.

Human neediness is double edged: it gives rise to joy when it is satisfied, and misery when it is not. This is duality. The Buddhist response to duality is equanimity. Salvation in Buddhist terms is open to anyone who is prepared to work for it. That work involves working on one's own self in the present. How present one is in one's life is a skill that can be taught through mindfulness practice.

As a child I was brought up in the Christian tradition of Roman Catholicism, which might account for some of my more romantic flights of spiritual fancy. Quite early in life, however, I began to have serious doubts.

The God that I was brought up with, and required to believe in, seemed to me to be a fearful, vengeful and angry sort of God. He scared me. If I ever loved God, it was only because I was too scared not to. God was a bogeyman. Many of the priests, I was convinced, were bullies in one way or another, too. And no one appeared to practice what they preached. This was how I saw it as a child.

One incident, more than any other, seriously affected me and helped loosen the grip of a faith I did not choose. When I was about twelve years old I went on a visit with my grandmother one Sunday evening to see some friends of hers, an elderly unmarried brother and sister.

When we arrived, I became aware that something was not quite right. Everyone was talking in hushed voices, and a priest was hovering darkly in a side room. It transpired that the mother of the brother and sister was gravely ill. For some reason I was encouraged to go in to the sick room to see her, although I had never met her before. Reluctantly, I went in.

The sight that confronted me would have been piteous, if it had not been so frightening. I saw a half-raised and twisted figure that clung to the bed in a semi crouch, staring up at me with a wild eyed, terrified and emaciated expression. She was moaning incoherently through quivering, cracked lips.

Her expression of abject terror, starkly visible through matted grey hair was more damning to what little religious conviction I had, than any anti-religious sophistry. As young as I was, I intuitively knew that I was looking at someone who was more terrified of the damnation to come than approaching death. I knew then that I would have nothing to do with a religion that filled the heads of children with superstition from birth, and frightened old ladies at death.

In the Christian creation myth Adam and Eve fell from a condition of grace when they were ejected from the Garden of Eden. According to this story mankind has felt the burden of need ever since. Humanity's separation from the divine is a frequent subject of mediaeval and renaissance art. Kings, Popes, Princes, Cardinals and rich merchants are depicted, sumptuously robed, but ashen faced in supplication to the heavens.

Their spiritual suffering is evident, and the weight of original sin remorseless. The Christian approach involves the work of atonement, but the final judgement is ultimately Gods'. Man's separation from God is absolute, though he may bestow grace on the chosen few.

Buddhism, on the other hand, is inclined to be more democratic and proposes a more forgiving 'original purity'. Perhaps this is why so many Catholics are attracted to Buddhism. There is karma, but it is counterbalanced by the possibility of transformation in this life, rather than the solace of redemption in the next.

The influence of my early exposure to religion lasted well into my middle adult years. It was a dark and fearful influence, and very difficult to excise. It may have been that I was a nervous and fretful child, and predisposed to anxiety. But I do recollect that all the stuff about eternal hell fire, damnation, purgatory, etc. had a profound impact on my childish imagination.

It sank deep into my subconscious, instilling an exaggerated awareness and anxiety about my own mortality, sinful nature and the ultimate destination of my immortal soul. Of course I had no real idea what a soul looked like, but my vivid, childish imagination had conjured up an image of a kidney shaped object, blackened by the stain of original sin, that floated in the air just above my line of vision. It was about the size of a rugby ball.

My first attendance at an Ash Wednesday ceremony to receive the ashes of repentance left me feeling as if I had been marked for death. That black cross, inscribed for all to see on my forehead, bore witness to my hell-bound condition and singled me out as a likely candidate for divine retribution.

And, as if that wasn't bad enough, the protestant boys, who in most respects were indistinguishable from other boys, would now be able to spot me as a Catholic and give me a good beating before I reached home.

I remember running home that day from church as fast as my seven year old legs could carry me, desperate to get home before a bolt of lightning could reduce me to a pile of ash, or a gang of 'proddies' to a battered pulp. To my childish mind religion, fear and suffering were inextricably linked.

In Buddhism suffering is the precursor of enlightenment. Each one of us experiences dhukka in life. Dhukka is a Sanskrit word that is usually translated as suffering, but some scholars have suggested that it is closer in meaning to a sense of 'pervasive dissatisfaction'. We are, it seems, never satisfied.

44

Each one of us will have experienced at one time or another the sense that there is something missing in our lives. What is missing, of course, is a complete understanding of who we are and our connection to what Dürckheim calls the 'Ground of Being'. The separate 'I' in the world does not feel its vital connection to the plenitude of existence.

In her book, The Sovereignty of the Good, the late Iris Murdoch takes issue with how modern man is presented in some genres of European literature. Citing the novels of Sartre as an example, she argues that to present man *"as an isolated free thinker, monarch of all he surveys"*, is to fail to do justice to the moral nature of man, or adequately reflect our connection to the world and to each other. To see more clearly, Murdoch proposes, we need to develop the faculty of 'attention', which she defines as *"a just and loving gaze directed upon an individual reality."*

Our perception of ourselves and others is filtered through a maze of illusion and fantasy. The relentless internal talk, or monkey mind as Buddhists call it, is seldom still. We find it difficult to suspend judgement in our interactions with others, and our relations become strained. In sitting meditation we can learn to develop the faculty of attention and develop a non-judgemental awareness of ourselves, and extend that through our practice to others.

It takes time, but eventually we can learn how to let go of the jabbering monkey mind through the practice of mindfulness. Letting go is fully attending to what is right in front of our noses, moment by moment.

During a Zen retreat training is continuous. Everything is training – training in mindfulness. From rolling unsteadily out of one's futon at 5:30 in the morning, to gratefully crawling back into it at the end of a long day.

On one retreat there was an item on our schedule that was called 'social event'. Thirty minutes had been allocated to it before the last sitting period of the evening in the Meditation Hall. Usually I am not very interested in socialising for the sake of it, and I was sceptical about the occasion. I was also slightly curious about how it was going to work.

I was part of a group of four, which included one monk and two other male lay persons. We met up at the appointed place, next to a reception area. There was a book case, a coffee table with a few magazines placed neatly on top and some soft chairs. We greeted each other a little diffidently, but politely.

The monk, a man in his early thirties, introduced himself and explained the purpose of the event. It was to socialise. He qualified this by adding that it was still training, and that the principles of mindfulness would apply. He poured tea, and when we all had our drinks he sat back looking at each of us in a calm and engaging manner. He said nothing.

It seemed that no one knew what to say. I felt a little awkward and began looking around the room, casually picked up a magazine from the coffee table and began leafing through the pages. Very gently, but firmly, the monk asked me to put it down. He reiterated why we were there – to socialise.

Then something remarkable happened. We began talking. We talked easily in a pleasant and relaxed way about nothing in particular. It was completely natural, unforced and very satisfying. At the end of the session we made our way to the Meditation Hall for the final sitting of the evening. Normally, I would have been like a nodding donkey, fighting waves of sleep for the last half hour of the day. On that evening I sat with vigour and energy.

When training in Zen, particularly in a formal setting, there is no opportunity for distractions. Spending a week at a retreat helps us to realise just how little we attend to what is going on in our everyday lives. Most of the time we are distracted by something or other, and seldom focus fully on what is going on.

We literally crave distraction. If we find ourselves at a loose end, then we turn on the radio, the television, our MP3 player, the PC, anything that will occupy our time. The first hurdle encountered by beginners in meditation is their own dis-ease. Coming to terms with just how scattered we can be is not easy, and doing something about it - at least initially - can be effortful.

A friend once told me that driving to work normally took about an hour on the motorway. One evening, he had almost arrived home from work but had no recollection of having actually driven that distance. He realised, with a start, that for most of the journey his mind had been on other things. On a motorway! He was a policeman by profession.

Often when we are involved in one activity or another, we bring something additional or extraneous to the situation. Sometimes we don't bring enough. Getting it just right is an art - being present helps to get it right. Being fully present allows us to shed a lot of unnecessary baggage and attend to what is directly in front of us with a calm disposition and a clear mind.

In the practice of Aikido we learn to deal with one attack at a time, regardless of the number of attackers coming at us. We learn to be present, not in opposition to our training partners, but in relation to them. With appropriate training a 'no fighting' mind will develop as we learn to let go of duality.

A feeling of dynamic and relaxed calmness will become the basis of our practice and source of power. In time this will be carried out of the dojo and into our daily lives and society at large. Life itself will become our dojo.

We realise that life is the true test of the effectiveness of training, and that in reality there is no separation between the dojo or Zendo and everyday life. In Zen, when a monk leaves the monastery, he or she will enter a new phase of training, which in Japanese is called 'mujudo no taigen' – the cultivation of Buddha Nature in daily life.

Being fully present enables us to both utilise and sharpen our faculty of attention. Being present, moment by moment, is the first step to building a bridge between heaven and earth. Training under an experienced teacher can be helpful, but a teacher cannot give us what we already possess. A teacher can only point the way. The important work is the work we do ourselves:

Daiju visited the master Baso in China. Baso asked, *"What do you seek?"*

"Enlightenment," replied Daiju. *"You have your own treasure house. Why do you search outside?"* Baso asked.

Daiju inquired, *"Where is my treasure house?"* Baso answered, *"What you are asking is your treasure house."* Daiju was delighted!

Ever after he urged his friends, *"Open your own treasure house and use those treasures."*

Are We There Yet?

Riding the Ox Home

I have spoken to many people over the years who have expressed the view that Zen training or Aikido training has made them what they are, usually people who consider themselves successful in life.

But it seems to me that whether or not one regards oneself as a success or a failure is irrelevant. At either extreme lurks complacency or despondency, both symptoms of an underlying spiritual malaise.

We live in a time of mass popular culture, for good or ill. It is a time of instant celebrities; they come and go and their 'fifteen minutes of fame' is over all too soon. Individuals that we had never heard of a year ago are catapulted to fame on the back of a hugely popular television talent show.

We are not surprised when they publish their autobiography, in spite of the fact that they're just out of their teens. The popular media reinforces the belief that life is about winning and losing.

Of course it is good to be successful, and to receive all the affirmation and plaudits that come with it, but Zen is a way of non-attachment and Aikido is a way of non-resistance. Do practitioners of Zen and Aikido know something that the rest of us don't? If so, what could that be?

If I were to ask a Zen master what the meaning of life was, he might or might not answer me. He, or she – because there are Zen mistresses, too – might strike me (unlikely nowadays), or tell me to go away. I might get annoyed, and call them a silly old fool. They might agree.

The truth is they can't tell me anything. I have to find out first hand. If I do find out, can I tell anyone else? I'm not sure, but my intuition tells me that it would be unlikely.

Attachment and resistance pull us irrevocably into dualism and suffering. The practice of non-attachment and non-resistance, on the other hand, leads to a deep seated calmness and equanimity that transcends the 'shocks that flesh is heir to'. Equanimity enables us to regard success and failure, in the words of Rudyard Kipling, as "those twin impostors".

It was this quality of inner calm or tranquillity that first attracted Eugene Herrigel, author of *Zen and the Art of Archery*, to study Kyudo (Japanese archery) just after the Second World War.

But Herrigel struggled to comprehend that the purpose of his study was in hitting his own 'true nature' through 'not-doing', and not the target at the other end of the archery range. It was many years before he was able to release himself from judging his performance in terms of success or failure. He was caught in duality.

The offices of psychotherapists are full of successful people – and not only because they are among the few that can afford the fees. Though driven and ambitious, high achieving and talented, many successful individuals find that genuine contentment in life somehow eludes them.

Psychotherapists regularly report increased incidences of narcissistic disorders among professionals in their occupational Journals. Achievement is fine, but what next - more achievement? In the Sixties Bob Dylan sang somewhat prophetically in 'Love Minus Zero No Limit':

> *"Some speak of the future*
> *My love, she speaks softly*
> *Knows there's no success like failure*
> *And that failure's no success at all."*

Self-judgement, as distinct from self-assessment or self-evaluation, is at best a form of narcissism. Whether it expresses itself as self-valuing or self-devaluing is relatively unimportant. It is the same old game, whichever way one plays it. At worst, it is to take something seriously that has been misconstrued from the outset.

The myth of Narcissus illustrates the futility of trying to make 'self' the object of love, and we are reminded again of the tendency of Westerners to make an internal into an external.

To be caught betwixt and between is the dilemma of narcissism. Ever questing for the authentic, and ever fearful of the inauthentic, the narcissist in each of us is seldom at ease. Whether in relationship or in isolation the narcissist can never be truly satisfied.

Although there may be temporary pleasures in living through the vicarious admiration of others, this is always accompanied by an uneasy feeling that it won't last. Professional actors can readily identify with such states of emotional insecurity.

But we should not be too hard on the narcissist. Chronic narcissism is a serious form of mental instability, and those that suffer from it live in extreme anguish. An average level of narcissism is the norm for most of us, and we cannot do without it – it is part of nature's survival pack.

The 'appealing vulnerability' that is part of our makeup, which is at its cutest in babies and puppy dogs, wears a bit thinner as we get older. If we continue to trade in it as a commodity in everyday social interaction, it becomes a form of narcissistic manipulation that has limited value in most adult relationships. For children, it will secure a 'jeely-piece' (jam sandwich) at most doors, but in adulthood it will restrict spiritual and emotional growth and be destructive of relationships.

The narcissist is very much at home in the dark interior of the subconscious. Let a little light in and it becomes very uneasy, and like the aforementioned three year old, may become prone to temperamental outbursts.

The narcissist craves what it fears. It wants attention and adulation on the one hand, but it fears that too close a scrutiny might reveal its fundamental lack of substance on the other. This is the narcissistic dilemma. It is the 'goose in the bottle'.

For some people narcissism can be extremely painful. When unaware of its influence, it can be a bit like a thorn in a shoe - a mild discomfort, but not serious enough to warrant treatment. For others, it can become a life threatening disability that enforces acknowledgement and resolution. Taking off the shoe might seem an obvious solution, but this is not as easy as it might at first appear.

In some cases narcissism can lead to quite negative forms of behaviour, involving various forms of substance abuse, unwise and destructive relationships, and an overtly 'macho spirituality' that can impair one's Zen and Aikido training. This was certainly true in my experience, and I suspect that it is more common than we care to admit.

Narcissism lies at the heart of cultism, both for the 'blindly faithful', and the charismatic individuals leading them. Disruptive of true balance, it can lead to excessive dependence and a superficial veneer of self-protective arrogance that almost always degenerates into hostility towards others. This is just as true of large corporate bodies as it is of individuals or groups.

Herrigel's teacher of Kyudo alludes to the state of imbalance that can result in violence to our nature, while at the same time hinting at its cure:

"*We master archers say: with the upper end of the bow the archer pierces the sky; on the lower end, as though attached by a thread, hangs the earth. If the shot is loosed with a jerk there is a danger of the thread snapping. For purposeful and violent people the rift becomes final, and they are left in the awful centre, between heaven and earth*".

Archery, then, is a way to maintain the connection between heaven and earth, or mind body. It is also a way of personal liberation if the self can be mastered. This cannot, of course, be guaranteed since it depends more on the disposition of the student than the teacher.

In Shakespeare's Hamlet, the dark and brooding Prince of Denmark is caught up in that 'awful centre'. In between the extremes of being and non-being, he is inextricably bound up in what seems like the prospect of eternal torment:

"To be or not to be– that is the question:
Whether 'tis nobler in the mind to suffer
The slings and arrows of outrageous fortune,
Or to take arms against a sea of troubles
And, by opposing, end them."

But is there any real prospect of an end to suffering? Not in Hamlet's dark view of things; even death offers no soul's repose:

"To sleep, perchance to dream.
Ay, there's the rub,
For in that sleep of death what dreams may come,

When we have shuffled off this mortal coil,
Must give us pause."

Hamlet's famous soliloquy is one of a man unbalanced by grief. The natural balance of things was very important to the Elizabethans. Like the Japanese, in the same period of history, the Elizabethans viewed man as a miniature reflection of the divine, at least potentially.

In Elizabethan cosmology to lack harmony within oneself was to be out of accord with the divine, to be victim to the dark 'humours' of the 'infernal' region as opposed to the light of heavenly grace. In modern terms, Hamlet exhibits chronic self-devaluing narcissism:

"I am very proud, revengeful, ambitious;
with more offences at my beck,
than I have thoughts to put them in,
imagination to give them shape,
or time to act them in.
What should such fellows as I do
crawling between heaven and earth?"

Herrigel's master archer might have said that Hamlet had 'snapped the thread', but the very fact that Hamlet was aware of what he was doing suggests the possibility of transformation and redemption. While many of us can attest that adversity and difficulty can promote personal growth - 'iron in the soul' - others can be completely overwhelmed by their own vulnerability. Tragically, for Hamlet, as the light of understanding begins to dawn his life is already drawing to a close.

Hamlet cannot find equanimity. He is in opposition to everything and everyone around him. He resists the way of the world and, more foolishly from an Elizabethan perspective, the dictates of blind fortune. Those that cannot accord with the turning of Fortune's Wheel must be taken by it. Hamlet's non-acceptance and rage may be an exercise in futility, but they are nevertheless common symptoms of bereavement.

Hamlet, if seen as Shakespeare's everyman, typifies a dualistic view of life in which humanity views itself in opposition to the world, as an isolated object "crawling between heaven and earth." But the important point here is that Shakespeare's Hamlet is a man in extremis, someone sick and out of balance. Perhaps he presaged the shape of things to come.

Some decades later a new age was to begin and Cartesian dualism heralded the 'new enlightenment' in Europe, paving the way for a rationalist world view that was to build a brave new world.

We have moved in a few hundred years from a Renaissance geocentric view of the universe to one that is anthropocentric. Modern man has gone to the moon, but are we any closer to living successfully with our neighbours on *terra firma*?

After two World Wars and a protracted, uneasy peace, countless outbreaks of localised violence, genocide across the globe and environmental disasters looming in the future, are we to conclude that we are any nearer to solving the difficulties of human existence and mutual coexistence?

Or is humanity like a family on an outing, with heads popping up from the back seat every few miles asking in chorus, 'are we there yet?'

A friend of mine was going through a divorce. It was a painful experience for her – it was her third divorce. She experienced rejection, feelings of worthlessness, abandonment, and worst of all, she felt a failure. Sessions followed with a professional counsellor, and in time she began to feel better.

She met someone else and formed a new relationship. At the final counselling session, having worked through all of the negative emotions arising from her relationship breakdown and divorce, the counsellor tentatively asked if there was anything else that she could do to help her.

My friend said no, she felt much better now. She got on with her life, but both she and the counsellor knew that she had not 'moved on' in her life. The time for that had not arrived yet. Perhaps it would someday.

During the mid-morning tea break at a retreat, a young monk joined our company, a group of lay persons chatting. A member of our little cluster asked the monk directly if he had ever experienced enlightenment.

An expectant silence followed. Monks did not usually 'hang out' casually with civilians; they were as a rule much too busy and probably keen on avoiding questions like this. But we were all curious to hear his answer.

He thought about it, and seemed about to answer when he had a change of heart. *"No"*, he said. *"It's not something that I want to talk about, but I understand your question."* The conversation turned to other matters, with only a slight awkward aftertaste of collective embarrassment. We all felt that we had tried to take advantage of him in some way. He was probably used to it.

Later that day I was assigned a task by this same monk. He outlined the problem. The monastery had a large black Labrador, and he was quite young and boisterous. The difficulty was that the dog had a tendency to jump over the gate of the kitchen garden and make a bit of a mess.

My job was to find some way of preventing this. We discussed the situation and settled on a plan. We agreed that I would simply extend the height of the gate and this would discourage the dog's forays into the garden.

I was quite proud of my carpentry skills and made the job as neat as I could. It took a while to do, but I had completed it by the end of the days' work period. As I stood admiring my handiwork, the monk came to tell me to pack up and get ready for the evening meal. He showed no interest whatsoever in my work. I found myself getting irritated and brooded over the incident throughout the silent meal.

By the following evening I had forgotten all about it. The sun was beginning to go down, so I went for a brief walk before evening meditation. My route took me past the kitchen garden.

I heard a soft footfall behind me and turned. It was the young monk. He said hello and commented on what a nice evening it was. I agreed. All thoughts of the previous day had gone completely. He looked at the gate and complimented the work. I thanked him. He smiled and walked back towards the monastery.

I was grateful for his lesson. He didn't have to teach me anything, but he did. In the Zendo, some forty or so monks and lay people sat in silent meditation. One breath at a time, the thirty minute session passed. Are we there yet?

Often we think that there is somewhere we have to get to; we trick ourselves into thinking that we are lacking in some way and so crave completion. When we sit in meditation we can realise that there is no vehicle, no driver and no destination.

Empty is full, and full is empty. Morihei Ueshiba, towards the end of his life, declared that *"The great path is really no path at all."* But letting go is not easy. Sometimes we have to let go of 'letting go'.

Yamaoka Tesshu, the famous sword master and calligrapher, was studying with his Zen teacher. He said to his teacher that he finally understood that all was empty. His teacher struck him angrily. Tesshu was offended. *"If you are so empty"*, said his teacher, *"then show me who is offended."* He dismissed Tesshu, telling him to come back when he was less full of emptiness.

Hindsight is a double edged sword: it can make a fool out of a wise man, or a wise man out of a fool. If it has to be used - if at all - it is best used sparingly. Sometimes we can catch a glimpse in the present of how far we have come, or of how far we have to go. This can give us pause for thought, but such insights need not preoccupy us too much. The Sanskrit poet Kalidasa (353-420) put it very well in his poem, *'Look To This day'*:

> *"Look to this day:*
> *For it is life, the very life of life.*
> *In its brief course*
> *Lie all the verities and realities of your existence.*
> *The bliss of growth,*
> *The glory of action,*
> *The splendour of achievement*
> *Are but experiences of time.*
>
> *For yesterday is but a dream*
> *And tomorrow is only a vision;*
> *And today well-lived, makes Yesterday a dream of happiness*
> *And every tomorrow a vision of hope.*

Look well therefore to this day;
Such is the salutation to the ever-new dawn!"

The narcissistic self fears its own dissolution. But it need not. The powerful energy that comes from mind body unification floods the narcissist inside us with the light of love and compassion. Like a sugar surfeited wasp at the end of its season, it exits stage left dissolving in a flood of illumination.

Less is More

Ox Vanished, Herdsman Remaining

Sometimes we do more than we really have to. Not so long ago I had the good fortune to spend some time on a remote Scottish Island that was noted, amongst other things, for its peaceful and tranquil environment. The weather, however, was not so good.

Each day was marked by persistent rain and gale force winds. Even the locals found the weather depressing. Transport in the form of a vehicle and passenger ferry service was unable to keep to its timetable, and as a consequence basic supplies ran short.

During one of the infrequent lulls in the weather a ferry succeeded in crossing the stormy Hebridean Minch from the mainland – a trip of some seven hours – and delivered its cargo of much needed goods and a few hardy passengers. The goods were offloaded and the passengers disembarked just as the wind freshened. They had got there just in time.

As soon as the shelves in the local shops were filled, they were emptied almost as quickly. Some were lucky. Some were not. The island economy mirrored that of the mainland, conspicuous over consumption driven by competitive self-interest.

A common scenario during the winter months on a Hebridean island, far removed from the bustling hive of activity that is our modern day, consumer-based society where every day basic commodities are taken for granted. Different worlds, one might think. But it all depends on your point of view.

Once, in the remote past, it was a community bound together by mutual poverty, blood ties and the necessity of cooperation. From the seaboard side the black houses were indistinguishable from the barren rock and heather of the hillsides on which they were rooted. Only the thinnest wisp of smoke could betray the warmth of hearth and human heart to a passing Norse or Irish marauder.

In the more recent past, the community was blighted by a series of events beyond their control. Potato famine carried in the air by the prevailing south westerly winds, was soon followed by the immigration of the young and healthy in search of a new life across the Western Atlantic.

The first European Great War and tuberculosis further reduced the population to the very edge of sustainability. The old and sickly remained behind. It is a community still on the edge, subsisting through government support and tourism.

It is an island of extremes, of contrasts and opposites. People come from the mainland in search of some sort of purity and simplicity - cultural, environmental and spiritual. It is a yin yang sort of an island, where seekers of the absolute crash in disappointment on the rocks of relativity.

It is also like anywhere else in the world - and many of its inhabitants have been all over the world. It is a microcosm of the earth itself, a miniature world. It is home to some 1500 people. It is a little mirror in which we can see our own face.

Every winter the locals on the island batten down their hatches as they wait for the promise of spring and fresh life, and 'visitors'. A community that once harvested the 'silver darlings' (herring), which passed with seasonal regularity as they followed the Gulf Stream, now cast their nets for a different catch. April to September is the season of the tourist.

The herring have gone, of course, over fished by the fleets of vessels that once crowded the island's main harbour. Now only the old savour the delicate, oily flesh that was once as necessary to life as air. Today's youngsters prefer convenience and 'take away' food.

Winter is long and drawn out and is a time when the old feel their age most keenly, and young people dream of life on the mainland. Strangers on the island are viewed with open curiosity at this time of the year.

Social life in the winter months, such as it is, centres on the necessities of work, basic shopping for groceries, Church and the occasional wedding, funeral or christening. There is a little fishing, and even less agriculture.

Incoming migrants from the mainland, seduced by the beauty of a summer past, queue at the local surgery for medication to help them through their first winter. There are other outlets, too, for those that prefer self-medication. Many do.

Some locals refer to their island home as the 'rock', which is basically what it is when all romantic associations are stripped away.

In the summer months it comes alive and the island is populated with 'visitors' and returning children with children of their own, home from cities on the mainland to visit their ageing parents. But in the winter it can be so bleak that even the seagulls go elsewhere.

Of course there is no such thing as a tranquil island. It is simply an advertising copy writers' device to sell holidays. The transferred epithet transports our jaded and stressed sensibilities into fantasy land. We are easily persuaded and buy.

Do we really think that we can buy tranquillity by exchanging one geographical location for another? Judging by the money we spend, and by the efforts of marketing companies, it would seem that we do.

In times gone by life was different in the islands. There were relatively few consumer luxuries, and most of the day would go by without even sighting a motor vehicle. The post office van, a red Morris, could be heard a good ten minutes before its arrival.

Not only did the postman bring mail, but he also brought news of people, events and gossip. He came with the smell of old leather and diesel. Children and dogs would be drawn to his van like gulls to a ploughing tractor. There was no hurry and plenty of time.

It's different now. There's more hurry and less time. The descendants of Norse raiders and Irish pirates still inhabit the islands, but they have a thoroughly modern sensibility and suffer from the same stress and life style ailments as their mainland counterparts. And it has taken a little less than three generations. It seems that the more we have of some things, the less we have of others.

What the island can offer the visitor in winter is a certain raw, natural beauty and solitude. But tranquillity is not supplied. You must bring your own. To go to an island that is full of solitude and lacking in distraction without some inner resources, is a recipe for a testing time.

Tranquillity is not an object. We can't go anywhere to find it. If we are looking for it, then it is only because we don't have it. If we can truly understand this, and accept it as a fact, then we might be able to experience what it is like. It is not stoicism.

Putting up with things without complaint is a form of 'macho spirituality' that will not lead to tranquillity; stoicism may arise out of inner calm, but it will not lead to it. When someone begins to practice meditation they encounter their own discomfort, their lack of ease within themselves.

This is normal and natural. From the perspective of sitting mindfully in meditation, tranquillity is never any further away than the tip of one's nose. It will come with time. There is no need to look for it. The less we look for it, the more it is apparent.

When we enter the dojo to practice Aikido we bow. We bow, not only out of respect for the environment in which we practice, but also out of gratitude for the opportunity to practice. Bowing is an important part of Aikido and should be done respectfully. Bowing in a casual, haphazard way is a waste of time.

When we bow wholeheartedly we are being most fully ourselves, and not just aping the behaviour of a different culture in an imitative quest for authenticity. Making it more Japanese, does not make it more real.

When bowing we are already beginning to practice, and it is the first step in casting to one side the dualism inherent in everyday life, our attachments, conflicts, anxieties, self-importance and desires.

In bowing we are acknowledging the reality of our connection with everything around us. In this one simple act we are already emptying ourselves and engaging with the energy of the universe. It is better to not bow at all, than to bow without the right feeling. Bowing is a marvellous opportunity.

"Bowing is a very serious practice. You should be prepared to bow, even in your last moment. Even though it is impossible to get rid of our self-centred desires, we have to do it. Our true nature wants us to." Shunryu Suzuki.

When we practice Aikido the dojo, the mat and our partners are all potential teachers. If we are competitive, aggressive or domineering, egotistical or arrogant, people pleasing or excessively passive, we can see this; how we are in our daily lives is reflected in our practice.

In the context of training in Zen and Aikido, the principles of competitive self-interest and conspicuous consumption are simply not applicable. We do not improve by training with greater frequency, by putting in more time and effort, but through sincerity.

Nor do we improve by looking for a return in our investment of time and energy. We are what we practice. If we practice in a greedy or acquisitive manner, then that is what improves. If we practice being hungry for enlightenment, then that is what we become.

It took Herrigel a long time before he understood what his teacher meant by being purposeless. In Japan students never question their teachers. They trust them and simply turn up for training. They understand that their teacher knows all about mind body matters, and that he understands them as individuals probably better than they do themselves. This is difficult for the average Westerner to understand.

When we practice with the right attitude, even when we might not feel like it - perhaps after a hard day or at a time when we feel at low ebb - we are surprised that we can enjoy it and actually feel better as a result. Conversely, when we practice with some particular result in mind we can be disappointed.

The reason that we feel good is because our true nature is appeased by practice. It understands what its needs and does not want any more than that. When we practice without ego our lower nature feels liberated by contact with our higher nature. This is the joy of practice.

In the practice of Aikido we often find that our technique is not working and we ask the teacher to come and show us what's wrong. More often than not we are doing too much. The teacher shows us how to do it correctly. Oh, so that's it! The teacher moves on. A few minutes later we are having problems - Sensei!

Sometimes it seems that the simplest things are the most difficult to understand. We are so accustomed to instant gratification, to largesse and conspicuous consumption that we are inclined to pass over that which is not immediately apparent. Much of the movements in Aikido are subtle and refined, and it takes time for one's faculty of attention to be become adequately attuned.

The frame of one's mind, which is narrowed through the pursuit of self-interest and over consumption, and reinforced by a culture and society regulated through those principles, takes time to free itself from its habitual mode of consciousness.

In time, however, we can come to realise that true power comes from 'not doing' so much. By and by we learn the feeling of relaxation and energy that comes from the mind body connection, of minimum effort and maximum efficiency.

The ordinary and the extraordinary are not separate. What we often overlook and take for granted, or regard as uninteresting and mundane, can in fact be very rewarding. This bag of bones, for example, this body that we spend our lives fretting over, obsessing over, or neglecting, is an amazingly complex instrument. When it is connected to mind its potential increases and we can do more with less physical effort.

To get some idea of what this feels like, the following exercise will help. It comes from a confidence building seminar that I attended some years ago, and requires two people to complete the exercise. It is based on principles that can be found in Chi Gong, Aikido and other mind body practices. It is designed to provide a practical example of what a positive, confident and relaxed frame of mind and body feels like. Anyone can do it.

One person stands with their feet shoulder width apart, arms extended to the sides in line with their shoulders at a 90 degree angle to their body. While standing in this way, the person silently engages in negative self-talk: "I'm hopeless, ugly, can't do a thing right," etc. The other person stands behind the first and pushes down on both of their outstretched arms, just above the elbows. The arms go down easily.

The exercise is repeated. But this time the person relaxes and engages in silent positive self-talk: "I'm wonderful, valuable, loving and warm hearted," etc. At the same time they visualise energy being drawn up from the earth or floor, through their feet, legs, torso, shoulders, along their outstretched arms and out through their fingers.

With each inhalation energy comes into the body, and with each exhalation the energy goes out in a continuous cycle. The other person then tries to push their arms down as before. With practice the arms will be immovable.

With regular training exercises such as these can lead to the development of a strong mind body connection. With practice the need for positive self talk and visualisation will be replaced by a 'feeling' that can be recalled at will. In the East this energy is called Chi (Ki in Japan). When mind and body are working together without physical strain, confidence arises naturally.

In modern day Japan mind body principles contained in the Samurai arts are being rediscovered and applied in areas as diverse as nursing and patient care, modern dance, and sporting activities. Japanese teachers such as Akira Hino, Yoshinori Kono and Kenji Ushiro regularly conduct seminars in both Europe and the United States. Students attend from a wide range of backgrounds, both martial and non-martial. Essentially they are teaching a way of achieving more with less effort.

To build a bridge between heaven and earth is to create a strong foundation of living calmness. When we act from this base life becomes less difficult. Actions that stem from this source have the quality of what is called Mu-Shin (no mind) in Japanese. In Chinese it is called Wu Wei – not doing.

It is a way of behaving naturally without unnecessary effort. We do not need to go anywhere to find it. The dojo or Zendo is a good place to start, but we need to be careful about what we bring with us. Having a good teacher – though not always easy to find – is also very important.

The Energy Body

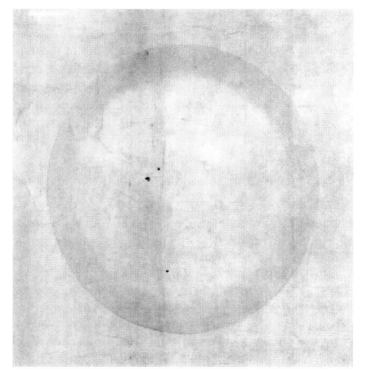

Ox and Herdsman Vanished

The roots of Qigong (pronounced 'chee gung'), according to anthropologists, can be traced back several thousand years to the Shamanic practices of nomadic peoples who inhabited Northern Asia and the Ural Altaic region.

The Anma arts, a form of body energy work combining acupressure, massage, manipulation and bone-setting, predate Reiki and Shiatsu by some 3000 years. Originating in China, the Anma arts spread from Korea to Japan where they became a specialised skill of retired Jujutsu practitioners. Albinos were said to be particularly gifted in its use, and it was also an integral part of a Zen monk's medical training. Such practices are still extant today among the Sakha (Yakut), Chukchi, and Evenki peoples of Siberia.

Core Shamanistic beliefs, which include body forms derived from dance, breath work, trance inducing techniques, animistic and polytheistic beliefs and myths, art, music and images and symbols were all assimilated by other major cultural and religious movements like Buddhism (India), Taoism (China) and Shinto (Japan).

Within ancient pre-literate cultures a Shaman was an individual, usually someone with certain unique characteristics, who stood out from among the other members of their tribe or society. They could be left handed, epileptic or even of indeterminate gender. Often Shamans would be associated with particular families that passed on certain genetically inherited traits, such as a physical disability.

Shamans were identified at birth, and although they could resist the designation, it was generally understood that in time they would come to accept the responsibilities of their role within tribal society. It has been reported by some anthropologists that individuals who resisted their Shamanic calling actually intensified their suffering as a result.

Often this resistance would be accompanied by prolonged bouts of illness, which could range from mild depression, physical and psychosomatic conditions, to severe psychotic episodes. Their eventual acceptance of their Shamanic role, however, was often preceded by a life transforming event or series of trials over which the individual Shaman had little control.

Typically this would involve falling into a death like state or trance, undergoing transcendent or realistic ordeals, and re-emerging into the world of light where the distinction between matter and spirit no longer subsisted. The Shaman, as well as being an ordinary human being, also had an existence as an energy or spirit body, and were able to pass from one realm to another at will.

The role of the Shaman within any given tribe or group was that of a healer, diviner, counsellor, or sorcerer, and they often acted as an intermediary with the "other world" on behalf of the tribe or individuals. The word "Shaman" comes from the Manchu-Tungu (sub-family of the Altaic language family) word šaman, and is formed from the verb ša – *"to know."* It means literally *"one who knows."*

In his book, *Shamanism: Archaic Techniques of Ecstasy*, internationally renowned religious historian Mircea Eliade concludes that Shamanism is the foundation for all the world's spiritual traditions. Eliade argues that there is a recurring motif of 'centre point' in many so-called primitive cultures, often symbolised by a tree that acts as a bridge between the different planes of existence. A Shaman is one who is able to climb the 'tree of the world', uniting the sacred and profane, the material and spiritual.

To accomplish this, the Shaman will have developed the capacity to go into a death-like state at will, from which he/she will return with renewed vigour and power as if reborn. This ability elevates the Shaman above the normal run of people, as one who is able to return to the source of all life at will.

The Shaman personifies the transcendent in their capacity to unite the sacred and profane within their own transformed existence. This notion of a sacred self being revealed through the extinction of a profane or worldly self is continued in Taoist, Buddhist and in the Shinto inspired belief of Morihei Ueshiba.

Tenchi: Building a Bridge Between Heaven and Earth

Cosmological diagram on Shaman's drum

The figure shows an artist's reproduction of a Shaman's drum depicting a three-world cosmology. The vertical arrow is similar to the world tree symbol often found in Shamanic artefacts, which stands in the centre of the world. It unites the underworld, the earthly world and heaven. This presentation can be found on Shamanic drums of the Turks, Mongols and Tungusic peoples in Central Asia and Siberia. The image comes from a drawing of a Shaman's drum from a 1909-1913 ethnographical expedition in the South Siberian Altai Mountains, led by Anokhin Andrei Viktorovich.

Japanese Shinto is pre-eminently Shamanic in its origins, and retains many Shamanistic features in its rituals and fundamental beliefs. At the heart of Shinto are polytheistic beliefs in the mysterious and harmonising power (*musubi*) of the kami (gods or spirits), and how truthfully that is integrated in the behaviour of man (*makoto*).

Makoto is not a sensibility that can ordinarily be expressed in words, although it is something that can be sensed intuitively by the faithful. Intimately connected to this is the idea of middle-present (*naka-ima*), the view that the present moment is the very centre in the middle of all conceivable times. In order to take part fully in the eternal development of the world (*tsunagari*), Shintoists are required to live each moment as fully as possible.

In ethical terms, this means living in a way that is consistent with the revelation of the truthfulness of the kami in man, or magokoro, usually translated as true heart, or sincerity. It is a quality that

70

denotes the attitude of a person doing his best in his social relations, work and personal life. The ultimate source of such a life attitude stems from man's awareness of a divine nature or higher Self.

In Taoism, Buddhism, Shinto and Shamanism, the idea of unification with the 'generative principle' that governs the universe, is a fundamental belief they hold in common. Morihei Ueshiba, the Founder of Aikido, described his life mission and the purpose of Aikido in the following terms:

"Aikido is the way of misogi (purification) itself, the way to become Sarutahiko-no-O-Kami (generative principle) and stand on the Ame-no-Ukihashi (the bridge between heaven and earth). In other words, the skills of misogi are Aiki, the way of uniting heaven and earth, the way of world peace, the way of trying to perfect humanity, the way of the Kami, the way of the universe."

For Morihei Ueshiba, Aikido was patently much more than a martial art. It was a way of purification and personal transformation, in accord with the highest aspirations of other major East Asian belief systems. It was a way of realising one's connection with the divine through the practice of Budo. A precondition for realising this connection is the experience of one's true nature as being not other than the universe, the realisation that:

"The divine is not something high above us. It is in heaven, it is in earth, it is inside us."

Morihei Ueshiba

The Shaman, both ancient and modern, informs us of man's spiritual connection to the universe around us. The naka-ima is the Shamanic centre point from which heaven and earth can be bridged; the past and future are contained within this point. We can investigate this for ourselves should we decide to take that step. As Morihei Ueshiba reminds us:

"Everyone has a spirit that can be refined, a body that can be trained in some manner, a suitable path to follow. You are here to realize your inner divinity and manifest your innate enlightenment."

Nowadays, large corporations include stress busting techniques derived from ancient systems as part of everyday stress management practice, confidence building and interpersonal skills training. While the rattles, totems and drums of the traditional Shaman may be an anachronism today, many of the characteristics and skills of the Shaman are still very much in demand.

From the charismatic motivational speaker at corporate events, to the Feng Shui consultant helping to construct a modern office block, ancient beliefs still influence the modern world. In contemporary Japan, and in North America, Shinto priests provide rituals of purification and blessing on the opening of a new building and many other significant social and life events. The ancient is still very much with us in the present, though continually changing its form.

Modern psychology, by contrast, posits many theories about the nature of the self. Indeed, it could be argued that we are in a position to know more about ourselves than at any time in our history as a species. A brief visit to any book store will confirm that. But most of this knowledge is 'about' the self.

While some of this information can be useful - especially for those who wish to persuade us to buy something - much of it has the quality of built-in obsolescence. It has a limited shelf life. Theories come and go. Like most things, they are subject to changes in fashion. Everything has its season.

Marketers, of course, know this. They understand the dynamics of satisfaction and dissatisfaction. Major world religions have always understood this too, without the benefit of in-house psychologists. Manipulation has been around a long time.

Psychology is a tool, and like any tool it is only as good as its use. Whether that use is designed to relieve suffering, promote happiness or serve vested interests is often a question of power.

A government may make use of psychologists to design a campaign to manipulate public opinion to bring down a banana republic, or it might use those same 'influencing' techniques to promote a policy aimed at improving public health.

All too frequently though, what we often see are politicians giving way to pharmaceutical lobbies to promote products that we don't actually need. The 'Bird Flu' scare, for example, succeeded in lining the pockets of some politicians whose links with those companies were less than altruistic.

Power can be used for our benefit or for our detriment. But what informs power and how do we learn to use it responsibly? As a child I was extremely curious. On one occasion, about the age of four, I clearly remember being fascinated by an old fashioned alarm clock, the kind with large noisy bells on top.

It had started ringing and drew my attention. Soon, I had it on the floor and in pieces. The problem was, I couldn't get it back together again and I couldn't figure out what it was about it that produced the ringing. I was looking for some mechanism inside that was responsible – the ghost in the machine.

Many years later, I remember reading the autobiography of Bertrand Russell in which he discussed his *Theory of Descriptions*. Earlier in his life he had been (1905) fascinated by the idea of logical atomism, the notion that the world can be described in terms of irreducible logical facts.

By breaking things down so that they could be reduced no further, primary causal connections could be established. One of his pupils, Ludwig Wittgenstein, later rejected this notion of logical atomism, and Russell also discarded it much later with some reluctance.

In his autobiography he commented that when breaking something down to its constituent atoms, it does not necessarily lead to a greater understanding of the whole. I can certainly vouch for that. At the age of four, I was a logical atomist and didn't know it.

To be able to use power responsibly one needs to understand who is using it. Politicians are occasionally caught out perpetrating or colluding in some corrupt practice or other, while maintaining an image of apparent respectability.

In reality they live on the blurred edges of legality and criminality. Usually such people have a distorted view of themselves and at heart are spiritually impoverished, having made a career out of insincerity and duplicity.

When we read about their activities in the press we are scandalised and outraged. But it is seldom the act itself that disturbs us so much.

We feel that we have been misled, that our trust has been betrayed and we have been let down. In short, we take it personally.

In a few days, however, we will have forgotten all about it. The scandal will be supplanted by another, perhaps more salacious news item. In all probability we will go through the same process again. This is how attachment works.

If we had been on holiday, vacationing in some out of the way place and read about these events at a later time, we would be much less moved by it all. That is how non-attachment works.

There is always a choice between disempowerment and empowerment. We may not be able to influence events, but we do have power over whether or not we are moved by them. We do not have to let our power leech out by getting caught up in the cycle of action and reaction.

In one corner of the dojo two burly students are resisting each other and struggling to do a basic technique. In another corner, an elderly lady with a placid manner is dispatching all comers with little effort. Who is more attached and who is more unattached? Who is the more powerful?

Some years ago, at an Aikido course held in the town hall of an English seaside resort, a local councillor came upstairs to complain about the noise from our practice. At the time we were having a short break. Apparently some loose plaster had been falling from the ceiling and was disrupting an important meeting being held in one of the chambers downstairs. Naturally we were to blame.

The councillor was met by a senior student that happened to be standing just outside the room where the class teacher was having some tea. The councillor immediately launched into a loud and pompous tirade.

Nonplussed by the irate councillor's demeanour the senior student remained polite and attentive. This, however, only infuriated the local dignitary even more who then demanded: *"Do you know who I am?"* The student, looking puzzled, opened the door of the teacher's room and said, *"Sensei, there's a man here who doesn't know who he is!"*

Who am I? This is the central question of Buddhism. Fear of confronting ourselves is the primary source of suffering. Release from suffering comes about through a non-judgemental awareness of the negative and destructive emotions that we all experience from time to time. Developing this kind of skilful awareness enables us to access and use power responsibly.

The logical atomism debate going on at the beginning of the twentieth century was in part a reaction to logical holism (the part can only be understood in relation to the whole), then fashionable in Edwardian England. It is, however, a much older debate as illustrated by Zeno's (490 - 430 BC) arrow paradox:

"If everything when it occupies an equal space is at rest, and if that which is in locomotion is always occupying such a space at any moment, the flying arrow is therefore motionless." (Aristotle's Physics)

In many ways it is a debate that is still current. The pendulum of intellectual fashion still swings between atomistic and holistic extremes, particularly in psychology. It has left us with a view of man broken down into his component parts at the mercy of his own history, complexes and phobias – a veritable Humpty Dumpty.

In reaction to this we have seen the growth of cults, internet and televised religion, alternative therapies, New Age oceanic movement's, weekend hippies and countless lifestyle gurus. One Zen master once described a seeker of the Way as being like a fish looking for water. But none of this is new.

Thousands of years ago the same atomist-holist debate was going on in ancient China amongst Taoist scholars and sages, but their predilection was for universal harmony that included relativistic ideas rather than opposing them. From the Chinese perspective – a civilisation that predates our Greco- Roman civilisation – the Tao was supreme.

To be at one with the Tao (primordial essence) was to be in accord with natural and universal principles. Within Taoism separation and unity are reconciled and opposites are brought together in accord with the Way of the Tao.

Through ascetic discipline and the cultivation of virtue (De in Chinese) man could realise his essential nature as none other than the Tao. The Chinese view of the nature of self is one of unlimited expansiveness. The Tao is the 'unnamed' and 'eternal' source of all power, represented by the Yin (female) and Yang (male) symbol.

Yin (black) Yang (white) symbol

When exported to the warring states of Japan, the influence of Taoism, now incorporated into Zen Buddhism, had a profound influence on the Samurai elite. It transformed their conception of power and how it should be used.

The sword was the 'soul' of the Samurai. Yagyu Munenori (1571 – 1646), a retainer of the Shogun Tokugawa Ieyasu and sword instructor to Ieyasu's son, Hidetada, was also a student of the Zen monk Takuan Soho. Around 1632 Munenori wrote a treatise entitled *The Life Giving Sword* (*Heiho kadensho*), that showed the profound influence of Zen teaching on swordsmanship.

The study of the sword is about becoming a man of the Way. The sword that can be used to kill can also be used to give life. The underlying philosophy comes directly from Takuan Soho's *'Unfettered Mind'*, which refers to eliminating the 'sickness' that comes from an excessive attention to technique and attachment to the idea of winning or losing.

For Munenori, the way of the sword was about self-discipline and a deep understanding of the principles of Zen. Study of the sword, therefore, was about freedom from attachment and liberation of the self:

"At the heart of this work is the idea that the sword that kills people can, on the contrary, become a sword that gives them life. In a chaotic society, many people are killed for no reason. The Death-dealing sword is used to bring a chaotic society under control; but once it has been done, cannot that same sword become a Life-Giving Sword?"

Yagyu Munenori.

The influence of Taoism is equally apparent in Shinto cosmology and in the writing and lectures of Morihei Ueshiba. When talking about Aiki, the Founder is known to have said:

"In this thing called Aiki, first describe a circle. Drawing a circle is, in other words, opposing powers." (Translation from Japanese text by Chris Li)

Here he is referring to the grand emptiness (circle), which in Taoist cosmology is where yin and yang (opposing forces) becomes manifest. Through the unification of mind and body (Ki) of man, heaven and earth are united. In this way man becomes one with the universe.

The Founder often spoke of *"Ichirei Shikon Sangen Hachiriki"* ("One Spirit, Four Souls, Three Origins and Eight Powers"), which represents a blend of traditional Shinto belief and Taoism.

In Shinto cosmology humans possess one spirit (*Ichirei*), four souls (*Shikon*), three origins (*Sangen*) and eight powers (*Hachiriki).* The four souls are the turbulent (*aramitama*), the tranquil (*nigimitama*), the happy (*sakimitama*) and the wondrous (*kushimitama*). The *"naohinomitama"* is the one spirit that acts as a container for the four souls.

The three origins (*Sangen*) denote the basic building blocks of the universe, which in Shinto cosmology are symbolised by the triangle, circle and square. These symbols in turn signify a divinely inspired template for life created by the Kami of heaven (*Amatsu*) and earth (*Kunitsu*).

This relates to the theory of 'Gogyo Gogen '(Rinzai Monk of the Zen Sect) where the elements of life - metal, fire, earth, wood, and water - are all shown to be transmutable and interrelated. Gas (triangle) can be a liquid (circle) and a solid (square), while a solid can become a liquid or a gas. They all have yin and yang qualities and each can transform into the other.

The Eight Powers (*Hachiriki*) correspond to four combinations of yin and yang opposites: moving - stilling, expanding - congealing, absorbing – loosening and combining – splitting. (See table below for comparison with Taoist cosmology)

In terms of Aikido technique the symbols represent the ways in which posture, breath and concentration (unified elements of spirit, mind body, Ki) interacts with the natural principles of the movement of the universe.

This in turn is condensed into physical posture (hanmi/triangle), spiralling movement (*kokyu*/circle) and the release of explosive power (*shunpatsu ryoku*/square [*Fa jin* in Chinese]). The various ways in which these fundamental natural principles can be combined and skilfully used can be ascribed to the sensibility of Aiki:

"Without touching with even one finger your opponent will be sent flying. Just to be able to do this one thing takes about 10 years. Let's try to advance quickly." (Translated by Chris Li)

Morihei Ueshiba

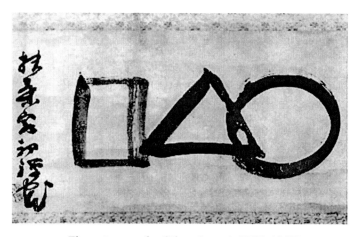

. The universe - by Gibon Sengai (1750-1837)

For the Founder of Aikido and many other teachers before him, both in China and Japan, the Taoist structure of the universe was a blueprint for establishing a mind body base and framework for the practice of Budo. The Eastern view of man is based upon a conception of a higher self that is not other than nature.

Man might be wayward and in need of discipline and correction at times, but nevertheless he is innately endowed with the potential for self-realisation. He is a universe in miniature and an agent of power.

The relationship between the numbers five and eight is important in Taoist cosmology. The numbers refer to the way that the five (wu xing) elements (metal, fire, earth, wood, and water) interact with the eight fundamental principles of the universe. Taken together the eight principles embody the philosophy of Taiji (literally the 'great pole'). Each one has a corresponding trigram made up of broken and unbroken lines, which are combinations of yin and yang: ☰ heaven = Yang. ☷ earth = Yin.

Taoist Structure of the Universe

乾 Qián ☰	兌 Duì ☱	離 Lí ☲	震 Zhèn ☳	巽 Xùn ☴	坎 Kǎn ☵	艮 Gèn ☶	坤 Kūn ☷
Heaven/Sky	Lake/Marsh	Fire	Thunder	Wind	Water	Mountain	Earth
Yang	Yang	Yang	Yin	Yang	Yin	Yin	Yin
Expanding	Congealing	Moving	Splitting	Loosening	Combining	Stilling	Absorbing

Eight principles corresponding with eight powers

The Water and Fire elements correspond directly with the Water and Fire trigrams. The element of Earth corresponds with both the trigrams of Earth and Mountain. The element of Wood corresponds with the trigrams of Wind and Thunder. The element of Metal corresponds with the trigrams of Heaven and Lake.

Chi (Ki in Japanese), according to the Yi Jing (Book of Changes 1122 B.C.) is the life force that enables all life in the universe to function. The 'gong' element of Qigong is simply the practical skills and knowledge developed by practitioners over time and passed from master to student down through the ages. Qigong is used to gather and store Chi to promote health, to channel and direct energy for the purpose of healing and promote spiritual growth and enlightenment for the individual practitioner.

The movement of Buddhism from India to China around 206 B.C. during the formative period of the Han Dynasty, helped lay the ethical groundwork for many spiritually oriented arts in China. This foundation was further reinforced by the Indian monk Bodhidarma ('Da Mo' in Chinese, 502-557 A.D.), who instituted a disciplined training regime at the now famous Shaolin Temple, located in East China on Mount Sung, in Honan Province. From there, this new style and approach spread to influence other martial arts throughout China and beyond.

While there are those who distinguish between Buddhist and Taoist influences in Qigong, viewing the latter as predating Buddhism, ultimately there proved to be more similarities than differences between the two religions. This resulted in a merging of the two that became known as Chan Buddhism in China, or Zen Buddhism in Japan and the West.

Zen was to go on to have a major influence on Japanese martial arts, complimenting earlier Japanese assimilations of Confucian ethics and Chinese classics and customs. In many ways, Japan's cultural relationship with China resembles European culture's relationship with classical Greece and Rome as the fountainhead of ideas and knowledge – Confucius was to the East what Aristotle was to the West.

Qigong is part of traditional Chinese medicine and incorporates Taoist, Buddhist, Confucian, martial arts and medical traditions. Within these traditions there are some 3,000 varieties. These break down into 'hard' or 'soft' types of Qigong. Soft Qigong is described as an "inner" variety, and 'hard' Qigong as an "outer" form, corresponding to the Taoist Yin Yang cosmological principle (In and Yo in Japanese).

As previously mentioned, the Asian martial arts present a view of mankind in which man is seen as a micro-version of the larger universe. Mankind is composed of five 'essential' elements (metal, water, fire, wood and earth). When these elements are in smooth interaction, and the relationship between Yin and Yang energy is balanced, then man is regarded as being in an optimum condition of physical and spiritual health.

Qigong consists of a series, or sets, of exercises emphasising posture, movement, breathing and visualisation carried out in a meditative and relaxed manner. The movements are slow and graceful and take considerable practice to perfect. They are exercises specifically designed to help develop the energy body.

One exercise, from the Eight Sections of Brocade (silk) series of movements that has particular affinities with the Tenchi Nage (heaven and earth throw) technique from the Aiki arts of Daito-ryu Aiki Jujutsu and Aikdo, is called Uniting Heaven and Earth. While not a throw, it nevertheless helps develop familiarity with whole body movement, energy cultivation and extension that underpins more martial applications.

It is an exercise that goes back, in various forms, to the Shaolin Lohan Qigong (the art of the breath of the enlightened ones) introduced by Bodhidarma. It is an exercise, like many 'internal' Qigong forms, that is designed for the cultivation of the 'three treasures' of jing (essence), qi (vital energy), and shen (spirit). Students of Aikido may recognise this exercise, albeit in a slightly different form, from exercises performed at the beginning and end of a typical Aikido class.

Uniting Heaven and Earth

The starting posture, wu ji (grand emptiness), consists of standing upright with the feet comfortably apart – neither too wide, nor too close together. The knees are 'soft' with the legs slightly bent, and never straight. The sacrum (tail bone) is slightly forward, pointing between the feet. The shoulders are kept relaxed and down. The head is balanced gently on the neck, with the chin drawn in slightly. The eyes are kept open, but gazing in an unfocussed way towards the distant horizon (*kan* in Japanese).

Breathing is carried out through the diaphragm (abdominal breathing), with the thoracic cage kept as still as possible. Inhalation is through the nose, and exhalation can be done with the mouth slightly open or closed. The arms are held loosely by the sides with the palms resting against the thighs.

Beginning with the hands, allow the palms to open to the front and let them drift lightly to the rear, while inhaling slowly through the nose. Visualise energy being drawn up through the feet, legs and into the perineum, then up into the spinal column to the front of the forehead. Next, beginning again with the hands, gently rotate the wrists to allow the hands to drift back to their starting point and rest against the thighs. At the same time visualise the breath as energy moving down the front of the body and settling in the dan tien (tanden in Japanese), an area just below the navel.

This opening and closing movement should be accomplished in one cycle of inhalation and exhalation. In order to coordinate concentration, posture and breathing with the movement of the hands, it will take several repetitions to develop a smooth, cyclical feeling of effortless movement. Once comfortable with the movement, then it is advisable to dispense with visualising energy. In sitting meditation, one soon becomes accustomed to the feeling of energy and composure after a few short breaths; it is the same in Qigong.

This first stage is about gathering the vital energy. The next stage involves raising the arms from the thighs, up the front of the body to just below the level of the shoulders. It is important that the arms are neither too far away from the body, nor too close – both extremes will result in an uncomfortable feeling of strain in the upper body, especially in the shoulder, deltoid and neck areas.

Starting from the hands, as in the first stage, paying attention to breathing and visualisation, allow the arms to gently rise with the palms facing upwards until the hands are just below the level of the shoulders. This should be done in one inhalation. Some people find it helpful to visualise raising a large ball of light (Chi ball), but should not be necessary if the first stage is practiced sufficiently.

On exhaling, rotate the wrists gently so that the palms are facing down and begin to slowly lower the arms. As the arms lower the hands will naturally begin to converge towards the centre of the body, coming to rest around the area of the solar plexus. Again it is important to use visualisation as in the first stage, imagining that the energy is moving down to the tanden. This movement should be completed in one exhalation.

As the hands come together just below the sternum, the right hand separates from the left and continues downwards (earth) to come to rest in the starting position. Simultaneously, the left hand begins to move upwards, rotating slightly so that the palm is facing upwards (heaven), accompanied by a fresh inhalation. The exercise is repeated, alternating left and right hands.

While performing these hand movements it is essential that the practitioner does not fixate on one hand or the other. Rather it is the feeling of contraction and expansion that occurs between the hands and around the body that is important. One useful image is to imagine that one is stretching an elastic (silk reeling) material that elongates or shrinks with the movement of the hands.

This movement can take considerable practice to perfect. Eventually, with practice, the movement of the arms becomes very light as if moving of their own volition with only the slightest intent on the part of the practitioner. A powerful feeling of energised relaxation, health and calmness comes from this exercise.

In order to understand the nature of our energy body the first step is the cultivation of mind body unification - unifying heaven and earth. The movements of Qigong and the kata of the Aiki arts can help to facilitate that process, as indeed can sitting meditation.

Without the sense of wholeness that comes from mind body unification, the movements of Qigong and the kata of the Aiki arts would be little more than choreographed movements, or techniques of manipulation involving physical strength. Learning to unite heaven and earth, as a practical application of an underlying spiritual principle, can provide the key to unlocking a resource of vitalising and powerful energy.

In ancient Taoism the relationship between the three treasures of man, jing, chi, and shen, was analogous to an alchemical process. Within this process an inner and outer alchemy were distinguished. While the outer form dealt with body movements and dietary preparations, the inner one was concerned with meditation and the cultivation of the energy body (chi). Although different, both forms were usually used in combination.

Jing is the primordial essence given to us at birth, sometimes described as the original chi. Chi is the universal life force, and shen is our spiritual self. In order to realise our true nature as a spiritual or energy body and transcend the cycle of birth and death, a continual refinement or development of the three energies was required.

To help us to achieve this, the ancient Taoists prescribed a formula that entailed using chi to nourish our jing energy, transforming the jing into refined chi, and using the refined chi to strengthen the shen. The ultimate purpose, of course, was the unification of shen (spirit) with the Tao.

Traditionally, there were a number of stages that a trainee would go through in order to achieve realisation. This varied from school to school, but broadly speaking they can be broken down into the following four parts.

Firstly, nourishing jing with chi involved carrying out exercises designed to cultivate chi energy, while at the same time living in a way that would reduce unnecessary energy expenditure. In practice this meant meditation to quiet the mind and passions, a healthy diet and moderate exercise or work.

Secondly, transforming the nourished jing energy into chi is a process of refining the jing energy so that it can be stored for use at a later time. At this stage it is much lighter and more accessible. Morihei Ueshiba, commenting on the nature of Ki (chi) in relation to Aikido, alludes to the distinction between unrefined and refined Ki:

"There are two types of Ki: ordinary Ki and true Ki. Ordinary Ki is coarse and heavy; true Ki is light and versatile. In order to perform well, you have to liberate yourself from ordinary Ki and permeate your organs with true Ki. That is the basis of powerful technique."

This second stage is often referred to as the 'water and fire' stage and implies an intensification of training in meditation. Water is our passions and sexual energy; fire is the intensity of our heart or intention (spiritual energy), which is contained in the cauldron of the dantien (tanden in Japanese).

As the imagery suggests, when water is above fire it will begin to boil and steam. As steam is light it begins to rise to the head. This same process can be found in the awakening method of Indian Kundalini Yoga. The Japanese ideogram for Ki is steaming rice.

In Taoism the practice is to bring the steam back down into the dantien. Like a cloud containing condensed water vapour, rain descends into the dantien (elixir farm in Chinese) where the heavenly chi and the earthly chi interact and mix. The environment that is created in the dantien through meditation practice is called the *"Reunion of Heaven and Earth."* The product of this union is the spiritual or energy body.

The third stage is likened to bringing up a child, and implies a period of extended education and protection of the spirit body until it reaches maturity. The fourth stage is returning to the Tao. In Buddhism this is equivalent to returning to the source.

Each belief system, from early Shamanism to modern day internet taught Buddhism, has its own particular language, images, symbols and mode of practice. The way of teaching may differ, but the subject matter remains the same.

The energy body or spirit exists in the *naka-ima*, in this present moment, in the exact centre of all possible times. It transcends the duality of past and future. It is eternal in its nature and quality. And we all have it.

An Eskimo Shaman of the Inuit people described his own conception of a higher nature (supreme Self) during an interview with an anthropologist in the following way:

"It is the supreme inhabitant or soul (inua) of the universe. All we know is that it has a gentle voice like a woman, a voice so fine and gentle that even children cannot become afraid. What it says is: 'be not afraid of the universe.'" Najagneq – Eskimo Shaman

Arising Naturally

Returning to the Source

The Founder of Aikido talked of "Takemusu Aiki", the spontaneous creation of form. It comes naturally from the study of basic technique. Basics are basics, but departing from basics and doing what comes naturally is frowned upon in many martial arts organisations. This is understandable, people doing just what they like all over the dojo mat would be unworkable.

But Aikido, like other martial arts, is constantly evolving. Change is not only inevitable, it is fundamentally necessary. It is built into the system. It is what makes Aikido a medium for personal transformation.

The organisational structure of Aikido is a vertical one, and is based on the 'trickle down' principle. That is, excellence and innovation are passed down through the hierarchical strata to the bottom.

Usually it works very well. Difficulties arise, however, when pressure, dissent or innovation comes from lower down. In Japan, it is expected and predictably they have a convention for its occurrence. It is called Shu-Ha-Ri (keeping the form, breaking the form, and departing from the form).

An experienced teacher, one who has gone through the process of Shu-Ha-Ri themselves, will identify its onset in their students. The teacher now has two choices, both of which can have a positive outcome.

The teacher can accommodate what is a pivotal point in their students' development and help them through it, incorporating whatever changes may emerge from the process into the system; or they agree that the changes are incompatible with what the teacher wants to do as a teacher, and they amicably part company.

Both are good, win-win results. In the former case the school or system benefits; in the latter, the teacher takes a proud interest in a new offshoot going out into the world to set up their own school or branch. In the West it is different. Few Western teachers have actually gone through the Shu-Ha-Ri stages of development, and people become teachers for very different reasons.

In Japan a student branching out on their own is usually the result of a very long apprenticeship, often not ending until the infirmity or death of their teacher. In the West students are encouraged to start up their own dojos with relatively little experience, and much less instruction than their Japanese counterparts. This Western 'fast track' approach has greatly assisted the rapid spread of Aikido throughout the US and Europe. But maturity takes far longer.

As one becomes more aware of the energy body, the practice of Aikido techniques and its prescribed forms will necessarily become more refined. Change is inevitable. The forms themselves may even change.

As Aikido is a way of non-resistance, this means that not only do we not resist our partners in training, but that we also accord with universal principles as they become apparent to us in our own training and development. We become aware of the teacher within and learn to trust ourselves and our insights. This is Shu-Ha-Ri.

In Aikido, as in life, there comes a time when we become responsible for our own development, and while this is a natural progression it can also be a very unsettling time for teachers and students alike.

Some students never reach this stage; they are content to follow living vicariously in the reflected light of a charismatic and skilled teacher, content to be directed; others forge boldly ahead, using the experience of past teachers as a source of inspiration and innovation. In between those extremes, there are many more whose practice is motivated by a myriad of different reasons.

Aikido reminds us that we are a universe in miniature. Within that universe we learn to build a bridge between heaven and earth. No one else can do this for us. This presents us with fresh learning opportunities and challenges. For serious practitioners of Aikido the day will come when they cannot rely on their teacher for guidance.

Each person's practice will mature and they will have to find their own way. This does not mean that they have no contact with their teachers, but both teachers and students have to learn to let go. Resisting this process is inimical to genuine growth, and can lead to endless frustration and disappointment.

In Zen Buddhism there is a story of a man hanging by his teeth from a branch jutting out from a cliff face. Nibbling away at the branch are two mice, one black and one white. A Zen master approaches the cliff edge, and bending down close to the unfortunate man says, *"And what is Zen?"*

If we are concerned about success or failure, we are caught up in dualistic thought and attachment, symbolised by the mice and branch. To understand is to let go. In order to let go, first we must realise that we are holding on. Usually we are holding on to fear of one kind or another, and fear generates resistance.

When I first began practicing Aikido I could not understand Ki. Training partners referred to it as if it was some sort of mystical quality that one came to comprehend in the fullness of time. What I felt, however, was mostly physical tension and brute strength, allied to the intent of flooring one's training partners. To win without fighting was a noble philosophical principle, but it was not something that was commonly understood at the time.

It seemed that few were able to appreciate the internal content of the form, so it was only natural for most practitioners to concentrate on the outward or objective form of the art. Things have changed somewhat, but this was how it was in the early days.

The Japanese, on the other hand, took Ki for granted and could not understand why we foreigners were so stiff. To compensate, they trained people to the point of physical exhaustion so that they could relax. Often this had the opposite effect, and many people simply became good at hard physical training. Nowadays there are a few Western teachers teaching Japanese Aikido students, but it took many years of dedicated and sustained effort to get there.

For the average Westerner training was all about technique, and it often looked like the ultimate object was to get someone down on the mat as efficiently as possible. Ki and subtlety would come, we were assured, at some obscure point in the future.

As I looked at my seniors, models of the future transformation that was to come, I had my doubts. Perhaps it happened for some, but not many. Most of us continued to practice in the hope or expectation of some future epiphany. But, as Sir Francis Bacon reminds us, "hope is a good breakfast, but a poor supper."

One Japanese teacher of Aikido had shrewdly observed that foreigners understood things differently. In Japan they accepted that mind and body were one. If you didn't recognise it now, it would come in time. In the West, on the other hand, foreigners were mind body dualists. Their mind-set got in the way and they were therefore unable to appreciate the true nature of Aikido.

In order to help Westerners better understand Aikido, this teacher developed a system of teaching and practice with the US market in mind. It was to prove hugely successful. But not all Japanese teachers approved. From the early 1970's the teaching of Aikido became polarised, with one style concentrating on Ki. The other main school, of course, had Ki as well, but they didn't talk about it so much – they were very traditional.

Attracted by this new approach, I began to practice a style of Aikido that focussed more on Ki. In lots of ways it was an excellent teaching system. It was a style that emphasised non-resistance, harmony and relaxation, and not just thumping someone down on the mat. It was definitely 'softer' compared to the 'hard' style I had studied previously, but something was missing.

It had a self-conscious quality to it that left me vaguely dissatisfied. But I persisted for many years with this style, and put my reservations to the back of my mind. What was missing, and ultimately what I was looking for, though I couldn't see it at the time, was naturalness.

Intuitively I felt that it was lacking. I was later to realise that naturalness was not something a teacher or style could pass on to their students – it comes from the 'teacher within'. I was also to understand that there were no shortcuts. Aikido, of whatever style, takes time to learn.

Since that time, I have had the good fortune to travel around the world practicing Aikido with many different people from many different styles and backgrounds. Occasionally, I have practiced with individuals who have this natural quality in their practice. It is unmistakable and a joy to experience. It has nothing to do with style. It is a quality that transcends stylistic considerations, national boundaries, gender, age and cultural differences. For me it is at the very heart of Aikido.

Everyone has Ki. Without it life would not be possible. But in the West we are not aware of it. When we become aware of it, we are inclined to view it as something other, an extra dimension or attribute that can be added to our personal resources. It becomes objectified. We think of it as a possession, something that we can get more of if we do the right things.

But Ki is not an object. In devising a new teaching model for Westerners this eminently skilled Japanese teacher had succeeded in turning an internal into an external. Yes, he understood perfectly how the Western mind worked and he constructed a rational system of teaching that made perfect sense and appealed to our need for clear explanations. But he replaced the empirical - finding out for one's self - with an article of faith: Mind Body is one.

Ki became a reified object. In order to understand the concept, it was necessary to suspend our dualistic mode of thinking. In the resulting intellectual void, a leap of faith was required to bring mind body back to its original unified condition, eventually. All over the world students of Ki could be seen, with intent expressions, self-consciously extending Ki. From a traditional perspective, from both Budo and Zen, the cart was well and truly before the horse.

Although there were clear principles and guidelines in place to help students understand and feel Ki, in reality it takes many years before this feeling of the energy body becomes a naturalised sensibility. If one has to think about the tanden and mind body connection, then it is not fully integrated. As one Japanese Aikido teacher put it, if it needs explaining you haven't got it.

In Zen there is a story that became the foundation of a well-known Koan (a prompt to help students attain realisation), which illustrates the difficulty inherent in too intellectual an approach. The story goes that a master came before his assembled students, and holding up a Hossu (fly whisk) demanded:

"Are you in the use of it or apart from the use? Who can say a word?"

Whichever way one answers - either in the affirmative or negative – one is caught up in dualistic thinking. It is the same with Ki. It is only through practice that one becomes accustomed to the nature of the energy body as not other than one's self. This is one of the reasons why repetition is so important in the Japanese approach to teaching.

In one sense, to say that we are learning Ki is almost nonsensical - we have always had it. Babies have it naturally. They don't require instruction on how to unify mind and body. To test this (if you are lucky enough to have a baby nearby) place your little finger in a baby's hand. It will enclose its fingers quite naturally around your finger. Now gently try and lift your arm and you will be surprised at just how powerfully the child can grip, with no apparent effort.

Unfortunately, as we grow older and become subject to the conditioning of a 'being-in-the-world' we lose this natural capacity, but it never goes away completely. Training in Aikido and many other arts can help us to recover a sensibility that remains obscured beneath the surface of our everyday consciousness.

Sometimes we can experience this in occasional 'Ah Ha' moments in our daily lives. A task that we had not completed, or had been procrastinating over, is suddenly accomplished without effort. "That was easy", we might say, but when we try to deliberately reproduce the same result it doesn't quite work out.

We know that we did it, but we don't understand how. We scratch our heads and move on. Some may even take the time to painstakingly reconstruct the entire process and develop a system that guarantees replication each time. But it is never the same. The freshness and vitality of the initial experience has gone.

What is happening and what enables us to experience this effortlessness, is something that I first came across in relation to my own Aikido practice more or less by accident. On occasions, when working on a particular technique, I would find that the technique would flow by itself with very little effort on my part. I did not understand it at the time, but little windows of 'not-doing' were beginning to open up. When I intentionally tried to reproduce it, invariably it wouldn't work.

Many years later, when teaching Aikido, I found that beginners could pick up this feeling of 'not-doing' far more easily than more experienced students. This was very curious. It seemed to turn the traditional learning model on its head. Why should novices be able to do something that more advanced students had great difficulty in doing? There was something other going on than just beginner's luck. What could it be?

A few years ago, while on a trip to Tokyo, I attended the class of a high ranking Japanese teacher of Aikido. It was a small class with only a few students in attendance. Among the students, there was a young female who was attending training for the first time.

The class consisted of exercises designed to help coordinate mind and body with an element of testing. Surprisingly, this young woman had no difficulty at all, and passed all of the tests with ease.

After the class, the teacher's higher grade students remarked on how well she had done, considering that she was a total beginner. The teacher looked at the young woman, smiled broadly at her in approval and said, *"Empty is full and full is empty"*. He then glanced at us, but he wasn't smiling.

In normal circumstances training follows a certain pattern. There is a definite learning curve which begins at a base of unconscious incompetence, rising to unconscious competence. Progress between those extremes is determined by many variables, some of which will certainly include personal commitment, quality of teaching, and opportunities for regular practice.

True learning begins with conscious incompetence. We learn from our mistakes. At this level the reflective action of consciousness is vitally important. The next level, conscious competence, is where most difficulty arises.

The reflective nature of our consciousness can actually keep us stuck at this point, unable to move on. Convinced of our ability and achievements, supremely confident in our understanding, and perhaps dismissive of others, we are nevertheless unable to move beyond a plateau of complacency that inevitably leads to dissatisfaction.

The goose is stuck in the bottle. From here, paradoxically, the only way up is down. If we are honest with ourselves, we can see that we are now back to the level of unconscious incompetence – we don't know that we don't know. When we understand and can accept this we can move on to the next level of conscious incompetence – knowing that we don't know.

When we come to the next stage again, of conscious competence, if we haven't adequately learned what it is about ourselves that holds us back then the process will have to be repeated until we do. For most of us this is unavoidable. Like the raw steel in the hands of a master sword maker we are base material in the process of transformation. This is misogi, or purification.

Training in Aikido and Zen, and in many forms of Budo, is a process of continual refinement. It is a lifelong training:

"Iron is full of impurities that weaken it; through forging, it becomes steel and is transformed into a razor-sharp sword. Human beings develop in the same fashion."

Morihei Ueshiba

This 'don't know mind' is very important in both Zen and Aikido training. It also helps to explain why novices in Aikido technique pick up the feeling of not-doing so easily – there is no mind clutter.

Beginners in Aikido are not usually impeded by a self-conscious notion of technical correctness, that comes later. But when they try to reproduce a technique with the same degree of effortlessness as before, they discover that it is not so easy the second time around. Why should this be?

They seem to have lost that original spontaneous and natural quality, but can't quite work out where it went or even where it came from in the first place – how baffling! It may be some time before they rediscover it again. The contest between self and no-self has begun. A process of refinement has started.

The 'don't know mind' is easily displaced by the habitual narcissistic tendencies of our egocentric consciousness, which wants to view itself as an object and others as foils in its own fantasy projection. It can take some time for this narcissistic impediment to learning to be resolved, and will naturally vary from person to person and from level to level.

Moving up the grades in Aikido does not guarantee escape from the worst effects of narcissism, or provide a warranty against its excesses. Progress in this respect is a matter of individual conscience and choice. But training in Aikido does provide many opportunities for personal development.

Apart from learning basic technique, there is something else going on that is common to all styles of Aikido: a re-conditioning and relaxing of the physical body and development of the energy body, or Ki. This dual conditioning goes on unseen. In fact it is encrypted into the kata of Aikido. A good teacher understands this.

This is true of other related forms of training, too. It is contained in the shikan taza of Soto Zen, 'just sitting'. In operation, it is the 'It that shot"'in Herrigel's Zen and the Art of Archery, the still point at the centre of effortless power in Aikido and the positive Samadhi of mind body 'dropped off' in the daily life of the Zen adherent.

The product of this conditioning is a quality of mind that is no-mind (mu shin), but it is not something that one can actively seek. It arises of itself through training.

In Japan candidates for the rank of Hanshi (8th dan) in Kyudo (archery) and Iaido (sword) are often in their seventies. The success rate is less than one percent. The slightest trace of self-consciousness will result in failure. It is a sobering thought, but instructive for people obsessed with grading and ranking.

Through training the body learns to adopt an improved posture that in time will become natural. Concentration and breathing improves and becomes more efficient. The body relaxes. Calmness develops and is increasingly present in the midst of activity. Ki flows from the energy body without effort, together with a feeling of well-being and respect for others.

In a very real sense, training takes us from the beginning back to the beginning, because there is no end. It is an opportunity for us to resume our true nature. It has never gone away. It arises naturally from the unification of heaven and earth.

Selling Water by the River

Entering the Marketplace

There is a story in Zen literature of two people meeting by the banks of a river. One is a passing traveller, and the other is a Zen master. When the traveller asked what he was doing there, the Zen master replied: *"selling water by the river"*. Teaching the power of Ki energy is like this. Ki is everywhere and freely available. A teacher cannot give Ki to someone. We have it already, but remain unaware of its potential.

Training in Aikido, and many other Budo arts, is a way to unlock this latent power. But one has to learn to get one's self out of the picture, and not get in the way. This can be very problematic, especially if you want to be powerful and have a competitive disposition.

Several years ago, during a break in training at a Seminar in Denmark taught by an elderly Japanese gentleman, I asked if he taught Ki. He looked at me in a thoughtful way and replied, "that's a tricky question." And that was all. He said no more. At the time I thought he was being typically Japanese and evading the question.

Later on during training, however, I had occasion to grasp his wrist in the way that I had been taught ('with Ki'), holding softly without any physical force. He didn't move. He just looked at me calmly and inscrutably from his seated position, and waited.

I was not trying to stop his movement, but I was not giving him anything either. There was no need for him to do anything. Embarrassed, I gripped a little more tightly. His whole body moved very slightly and I felt a jolt pass through my body. I felt my head snap back as the energy travelled the length of my body, and the next thing I knew I was hurtling forward. By the time I landed he was already throwing the next person.

To get something you have to give something. It is in the nature of power to be reciprocal. This old man had come all the way from Japan – no mean feat at the age of eighty three – to help train foreigners. He wasn't teaching a one-size-fits-all approach, although in a formal sense what he was teaching was kata. But he adapted it to each individual. I noticed that he took the same approach with students that used a lot of physical strength – he simply waited until he was able to give them something, and they were ready to receive his lesson.

When we come to practice, often times we bring 'stuff' with us that just gets in the way. Learning to get out of our own way is what helps us to make progress. Sometimes it can be painfully slow.

What is appropriate in one context is not always useful in another. But we are creatures of habit, and regardless of where those habits come from they help us navigate through our lives. Teachers find it difficult to get through to students who refuse to switch off their auto pilot. But if we want to learn it is important to be open.

Being open means being willing to change. But changing the habits of a lifetime is not so easy. Learning to understand Ki is essentially about overcoming one's habitual mode of consciousness; it is not about getting rid of habits. That would be impossible. Instead, we learn to take on new habits of mind and body. This is the training. In time those unhelpful habits will be displaced by new, more helpful ones.

The first obstacle that we inevitably encounter is duality. Our teacher tells us that mind and body are one. This sounds great, but we find that duality is still there in spite of our best efforts. This is partly to do with our social and cultural conditioning, but it is mostly to do with how we develop as a 'being in the world'. In Buddhism this is referred to as the doctrine of dependent origination.

From a foetal environment in which everything is in perfect symbiotic harmony, to the experience of an external reality presents us with a stark juxtaposition from the very beginning. As we mature our sense of separateness is consolidated and reinforced by our social and cultural experience. This is normal, and without this process our survival would be in serious jeopardy.

But something of our origin, of that original experience of harmonious balance remains with us. As adults we try to recapture that natural suppleness given to us by nature, and lament our physical limitations.

Children are full of natural Ki, unless they have been maltreated in some way. They have not yet learned how to lose it. That comes with experience. To 'get' Ki is an oxymoron. There is nowhere to get it from. But it is possible to cultivate it through training. But it is never *your* Ki - it is of the universe.

Fight or flight seems to be our stock response to many of our everyday life situations, creating tension and stress, making each day a struggle - if not for material survival - then certainly to feel at home with ourselves, our neighbours, and with our environment.

Denial, blame and absorption in endless consumption and distractions do not assuage that pervasive sense of dissatisfaction that we can all feel from time to time. We all want to find happiness in our lives. We search, and if we find it at all, it's a fleeting, transient phenomenon – nothing seems to last for long.

Perhaps we need to change our approach. There are many forms of self-cultivation, cults and therapeutic regimes. Systems abound to cater for our numerous neuroses. There are many prescriptions for attaining that which we lack – so we are informed. Are we really so bereft or resources? George Bernard Shaw, commenting on the subject of happiness had this to say:

"We have no more right to consume happiness without producing it than to consume wealth without producing it."

We can change focus, shift the emphasis, and concentrate on the production of happiness rather than its consumption. If we find that we have some, then why not give it away? In this way there will be no shortage. All that is required is a starting point.

Unifying mind and body is a beginning. It is not an end. Conducting our daily lives with mind and body unified will enable us to utilise a power that is everywhere around us.

Mind and body unification is what enables us to feel and utilise Ki energy. The more we make use of it, the more we have to make use of. Learning to breathe with Ki is an efficient way to develop our 'Ki feeling', or energy body. And anyone can do it.

In any case we are already using Ki, and need only make it a more fully conscious and practical part of our lives. It is an effective antidote to the spiritual battering that accompanies everyday life, so well described by Boris Pasternak in his novel, *Doctor Zhivago*:

"The great majority of us are required to live a life of constant, systematic duplicity. Your health is bound to be affected if, day after day, you say the opposite of what you feel, if you grovel before what you dislike and rejoice at what brings you nothing but misfortune. Our nervous system isn't just a fiction, it's a part of our physical body, and our soul exists in space and inside us, like the teeth in our mouth. It can't be forever violated with impunity."

One way to experience what mind body unification feels like is through the breath. Many of us take breathing for granted and fail to understand just how our breathing habits can affect our quality of life. Changing our breathing can change us.

Breathing is often something that we don't do well, yet it is perhaps the easiest way to begin to develop Ki. The majority of us, unless we are trained musicians, singers or athletes, breathe in an inefficient way and fail to benefit fully from this most essential and natural of functions.

Our habitual breathing is usually shallow chest breathing and employs a limited range of muscles confined to the thoracic cage, upper chest and, often as a result of tension, the muscles of the neck and upper shoulders. This can result in tension headaches and feelings of lethargy. By changing how we breathe, it's possible to change how we feel.

Ki or Chi Breathing

Ki (energy), or Chi in Chinese, is the vital energy that permeates the universe. In Asia and throughout the Indian sub-continent it has always been viewed as something that can be cultivated. Ki breathing, as described in the exercise that follows, is a form of training that was originally developed in Japan by Tempu Nakamura [7].

Many traditional arts in Japan, including the martial arts, the tea ceremony, calligraphy, Sumo wrestling, and many others, all involve the training of the breath, or 'kokyu' - breath power. The belly (Hara in Japanese) is very important in breathing. In Japan this kind of training is colloquially referred to as 'training the belly'.

Ki breathing is an exercise that is normally performed while seated in the traditional Japanese kneeling posture known as seiza [8]. It can also be practiced while standing or walking. Whether seated, standing, or in movement it is important to be relaxed. By expelling stale Ki and inhaling fresh Ki efficiently, we can invigorate both mind and body and increase the physical capacity of the respiratory function.

Posture

The practitioner should sit (a chair is fine) with the back straight, but not rigid. The shoulders should be down, and the head should rest lightly on the neck, with the chin slightly tucked in. The weight of the upper torso should be firmly anchored on top of the pelvis, and the hands resting gently on the upper thighs.

A good way to check body alignment is to let the sacrum (tail bone) arch backward slightly, and then straighten it - but not too tightly. The lower abdomen should feel full, but soft and relaxed. The more the upper body relaxes the fuller the lower abdomen will feel. Placing a firm cushion under the buttocks' (sitting bones) will help with the proper alignment of the pelvis and abdomen.

Breathing in and Breathing Out Exercise

There are basically two stages of inspiration for this exercise, and both are employed during the inspiratory phase of Ki breathing: abdominal and thoracic. Inhalation begins with inhaling through the nostrils in a slow, continuous movement, allowing the lower abdomen to inflate while keeping the thoracic cage as still as possible.

The second (thoracic) phase begins when the abdomen feels full. At this point continue to inhale by opening up the chest, allowing the upper part of the lungs to fill completely with air. After a brief pause of a few seconds holding the breath, exhalation begins.

Expiration is achieved by constricting the epiglottis, and letting the air out through parted lips in a thin stream, with an elongated 'AH' or 'HA' sound. At the end of the exhalation, when all of the breath seems to have left the lungs, by means of leaning slightly forwards the diaphragm pushes out the remainder or 'reserve volume' of breath - again with an 'AH' or 'HA' sound.

Remaining in this forward position, inhalation commences as in the beginning of the exercise. When the abdomen has been fully inflated one's upper body returns to an erect posture and thoracic breathing commences. This allows the external intercostals and the muscles of the neck to combine to lift the front of the thoracic cage and increase the depth of the pleural cavity, augmenting the amount of air into the lungs well above the tidal volume of normal breathing. The breath is then held for a few seconds, and released as the cycle begins again.

With practice this can develop into a flowing, rhythmical movement that can energise body and mind. To get full benefit from this exercise, ten to fifteen minutes each day should be enough. Be careful not to hold the breath too long. This exercise should be carried out at your own pace, with comfort and ease. Gasping is an indication that you are not getting it right.

Physiologically there are two main parts to the breathing process. On the one hand we need to consider the volume of air that can be taken into the lungs; and on the other, the physical mechanism that enables the activity of inspiration and expiration to take place.

The total lung capacity of the average person is on a scale of between ml.0 to 5700. At the very bottom of this scale, between ml.0 and 1200 millilitres, there is the so-called residual lung volume. This means that although all of the muscles of expiration are fully contracted, 1200 millilitres of air still remain in the lungs.

The reason for this is simply that no amount of physical exertion can collapse all of the alveoli and respiratory passages. This partially explains why, at the end of a long exhalation during the Ki breathing exercise, experienced practitioners can remain without being affected unduly by the need to gasp air into the lungs.

Normal respiration occurs between the levels of 2300-2800 millilitres, increasing to 2800 on inspiration and decreasing to 2300 on expiration. This is the range of normal breathing and is known, for obvious reasons, as the tidal volume.

At the end of expiration during the exercise it is possible through the contraction of the expiratory muscles - the abdominals and the internal intercostals - to expel an additional 1100 millilitres of air from the lungs.

Expiration in Ki breathing differs from normal breathing to the extent that not only does it go beyond the normal tidal volume, and down into what is known as the expiratory reserve volume, but it utilises the diaphragm in opposition to the natural upward movement of the viscera and the abdominal muscles. This produces a kind of bated or attenuated breath that can be expelled in a long continuous stream.

The interplay of these various muscles can be experienced very simply. All that is required is to sit 'seiza', letting the body relax completely and one's centre of gravity to settle naturally in the lower abdomen. With the mouth slightly open, air is expelled with an AH or HA sound, effectively constricting the epiglottis, and causing the diaphragm to strongly oppose the rising viscera.

At the end of the exhalation, when all of the breath seems to have left the lungs, by means of leaning slightly forwards the diaphragm is brought into stronger opposition and the expiratory reserve volume is expelled.

Ki breathing can help in many ways. This particular exercise helps develop powerful diaphragmatic breathing. On a physiological level it can also improve the supply of oxygenated blood to the major organs of the body, including the brain, heart, lungs, liver, kidneys, etc. It can improve the efficiency of elimination of waste matter and impurities from the body and it can help maintain the effective functioning of the autonomic nervous system.

Ki breathing helps to promote a calm and relaxed disposition in one's daily life, and assists the beleaguered sympathetic nervous system to recover naturally. The natural regenerative ability of the human body can reassert itself without the intervention of synthetic substances, which only hasten the deregulation of the autonomic system.

Ki arises as a feeling, and this is where it gets a little complex. It is a feeling that can be extended, directed and used in many different ways. In Japan Ki can refer to many subjective conditions and personality traits relating to mood, attitude and character – Ki qualities can even be ascribed to the condition of the weather.

For the Founder of Aikido man quite literally mirrored the divine structure of the universe, man was a microcosm of the divine. In this sense, Morihei Ueshiba could be regarded as a typical mystic seeing divine significance everywhere. He would have, in all probability, appreciated the romantic and mystical sensibilities of Blake's [9] poetry:

> *"To see a world in a grain of sand,*
> *And a heaven in a wild flower,*
> *Hold infinity in the palm of your hand,*
> *And eternity in an hour."*

But Blake was not only a mystic poet, he was also a skilled craftsman and artisan, and Morihei Ueshiba trained on a daily basis to perfect his art throughout his life. There is a very practical side to Ki that, while it can be explained within complex and abstract cosmological terms, remains very pragmatic and down to earth.

As one Zen sage put it, *"when pointing at the moon we must not mistake the finger for the moon."* Abstraction, though interesting, can take us down some obscure and confusing paths, and it is useful to bear in mind that there is a difference between 'knowing about' and 'knowing of' something. For training to be meaningful it has to suffuse our whole being.

Interestingly, Morihei Ueshiba often commented that when Aikido was performed well it could look as if it was being faked. The Daito-ryu teacher (and Morihei Ueshiba's teacher), Sokaku Takeda, was also known to have made similar remarks about his own art. Ultimately, experience gained through training helps us to understand that most of what is displayed outwardly comes from an unseen internal source:

"Form is empty and empty is form."

As Yamaoka Tesshu [10], the renowned Japanese Sword, Zen and Calligraphy Master reminds us, *"In order to understand if the water is hot or cold, first you must taste it"*. In a martial context, or indeed in a real life situation, one cannot defend oneself or one's family with an intellectual explanation.

Experience is of primary importance, and in the early stages repetition is a necessary part of training and understanding.

Yamaoka Tesshu uses a carpentry analogy to delineate the stages in training as: *"rough planing, smooth planing and fine planing."*

> *Spirit, swift*
> *Mind, calm*
> *Body, light*
> *Eyes, clear*
> *Technique, decisive!*
> (Doka, Yamaoka Tesshu)

For Morihei Ueshiba, man's place is in the centre uniting the 'high plain of heaven' (*Takamagahara*) and the earth. Man is designed by nature to be a unifying force. He is an agent of power and has the capacity to unite the opposing forces of yin and yang within his own existence and realise his true nature and power. Aikido and other forms of training are designed to help establish a mind and body that is capable of fulfilling man's divine purpose or mission – world peace and harmony.

The Ki of the universe is no different from the Ki of man, but in order to find his place in the universe man must first unify himself by bringing mind and body together. In order to do this, posture, breathing and attention (concentration) are cultivated to develop a strong, but relaxed body and calm mind capable of storing, directing and exchanging powerful energy.

At the same time the vital force, or Jiriki, that comes from training also permits the growth of compassion and wisdom to inform and guide the responsible use of power. Heaven and earth can be unified in a single human form; mind and body can be unified through the breath; and the breath of man is the breath of the universe.

Difficulty can arise, of course, where ego and wilfulness enter into the picture. An internal can be misconstrued as an external, and Ki can be regarded as something separate - as so much equipment in the service of the will. This can become a little thorny for students, but it can be fixed if the student has the right kind of motivation and with the right kind of training and guidance from a good teacher. The rest is about maturity.

Entering the market place, laden with goods and presents the enlightened person gives away all the contents of the huge sack he is carrying. With each step on his journey he is becoming lighter. Ki works in the same way. The more we extend, the more we are able to extend. This is the nature of power.

Yamaoka Tesshu, 1836 –1881

Epilogue - The Country of Fire

Although I had been to Japan many times when I was younger, it had never been in connection with Zen or Aikido. Mostly it was about work and associated recreational activities. Each stay was very short and I did not get to see much, apart from the neon illuminated night life. It was a time when Japan was at its economic peak and I was the proverbial horse playing in a large field.

Many years later, looking back and considering my particular interests, I couldn't help feeling that I had missed a tremendous opportunity – the folly of youth. But early in the summer of 2007, I received an invitation from an American with whom I had been corresponding who lived in Kumamoto. He invited me to attend an International Gasshuku [11] hosted by an Aikido organisation based in Kyushu, in the south of Japan. I couldn't believe my luck. I was genuinely surprised and delighted to be invited.

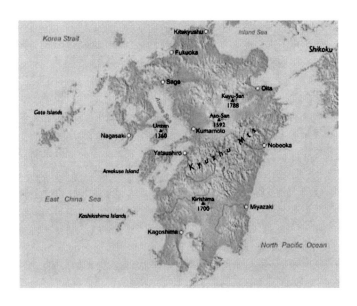

Western Students and Hamada Sensei and Mrs Hamada at Gasshuku

I was one of several foreigners drawn from various parts of the world, including the United States, Korea, Slovakia, France and the United Kingdom. For me it was the opportunity of a lifetime – a chance to go to Japan! I accepted immediately, once I had got permission from my wife.

At the age of fifty, with many years of experience of practicing Aikido, I set off for Japan from London via a connecting flight from Paris. After a gruelling fifteen hour flight I landed at Narita airport on the morning of the third of November, 2007- it felt like my first time in Japan.

I headed straight from the airport to my cut-price hostel in an inexpensive part of Tokyo – I had done my research - and from there straight to a class at Gakkshuen University Club, taught by an internationally renowned Aikido teacher.

I was like a child in a toy shop. In my enthusiasm I had no time for jet-lag. I only really noticed it when I came to a sudden stop at the top of an escalator, or when walking into bollards on the street. Japanese onlookers, I seem to remember, looked genuinely surprised, pained or puzzled at my odd behaviour. Some even looked impressed.

Did this jet-lagged feeling affect my Aikido practice? Of course it did, but I didn't mind. I was much too high on the excitement of the occasion and too much coffee to be overly concerned. I do remember the teacher taking me for ukemi [12] once, and throwing me away with a grunt of dismissal – I wasn't so much following as using him for support!

I had absolutely no reservations about being in Japan on my own, and besides I was accompanied by an old friend, scepticism. Not the kind that regards everything as questionable, but the open, curious kind that sustains and nourishes interest and passion.

I had come from a style of Aikido that was independent of Japanese influence, quite a large and thriving organisation based in Britain. But I had many questions that required answers, and I wanted to find out first hand if what I had been told about Japanese Aikido was true. I learned that most of it wasn't, and I was also to find out that, in spite of my many years of practice, I knew less than I thought I did. It was a reality check.

What would this organisation in the south really be like? Was I going to be disappointed? I had no idea. But I was certainly going to find out. I had come to Japan with the single minded intent of maximising learning opportunities. It was all about Aikido. I had come to feel something.

Ultimately, what I was to feel most strongly was the giving and selfless nature of the Japanese people, at all levels. From the ordinary workman who gifted me a bowl of noodles and tempura for breakfast in Tokyo, simply because I was a hungry guest in his country, to the veteran Aikidoka [13] with arthritic knees who taught me kokyu ho [14] exercises from a folding stool. And both with a pure delight in the act of giving without looking for anything in return.

I stayed in Tokyo for six days and attended Doshu's [15] early morning classes at Hombu [16] Dojo, as well as other classes taught by different Hombu teachers. I also met and had classes with the son of a well-known Aikido teacher. I had been in communication with him and had written to him requesting information about his late father's Aikido, which I admired. When he learned that I was coming to Japan he was kind enough to invite me to his private dojo, where I took part in a small class with a few of his students. I was the only foreigner.

I was really impressed with his Aikido and found him very friendly and approachable, as well as an excellent teacher. I felt very honoured to be his student, and learned a great deal from him in the little time that I was able to spend with him. On the sixth day I boarded the Bullet Train and headed south to Kumamoto.

Kumamoto, on the island of Kyushu in South Western Japan, 'the country of fire' from where the Founder of Aikido proclaimed his Budo would 'flourish', was to be my home for the next six days. And truly, I felt very much at home and was treated with a degree of courtesy and respect that made me feel like a welcomed guest.

The generosity and consideration shown by my hosts, and from complete strangers, too, on many occasions, have left a lasting impression on this 'gaijin san'. It was a humbling experience.

Here I was - I could scarcely believe it - at the Hombu Dojo in Kumamoto, standing on real tatami! And it was real, not the vinyl covered shock-absorbing material that I was accustomed to. It was made in the traditional way, from compacted rice straw. This material did not seem to have any give in it at all and seemed harder than the floor underneath. I suspected that it was designed to protect the floor, and not those landing on its surface.

Original calligraphy crafted by the Founder, at once boldly energetic and delicately whimsical, graced the timber cladded walls. The dark panelling was worn silky smooth by over a half century of 'sooji', the ritual cleaning and purification carried out before and after each practice.

My bed was on the tatami, too. Each night I rolled out my two futons (a kind concession) and drifted off to sleep fancying that I could hear the soft footfall of the Founder's tabi as he moved around checking that all was well. The Founder of Aikido made frequent trips around Japan, and had a circle of older students with whom he visited. This particular Dojo featured in many old newsreel and press photographs taken during his classes.

On the first morning I was awakened abruptly by a hollow booming sound that grew in tempo and intensity. As my eyes began to focus in the soft light, I gazed upwards towards the ceiling and I could just make out what looked like items of clothing hanging from the rafters. Confused and disorientated, I looked around and was reassured to see bodies shifting on neighbouring futons.

Memory flooded back and I realised with gratitude that I was not in some nightmarish laundry, but in the Kumamoto Dojo. The booming sound was in fact the drumming that came from the Shinto Jinja (temple) adjacent to the dojo on whose grounds the dojo was built. It was a sound that I came to sleep right through as our busy training schedule reduced me to near unconsciousness by bed time each night. The items of clothing were keikogi [17] suspended from a drying rail. At the end of each practice we hung our kit, neatly arranged to dry out for the next session.

A Japanese teacher led each practice. His name was Hamada Sensei (teacher). He was a kind and thoughtful host, and unusually tall for a Japanese person. I distinctly remember his forbearing attitude when I made some error in etiquette or displayed what might have appeared to be laziness or lack of spirit. In truth I was physically exhausted most of the time and my knees were a source of constant pain.

He led at a fast pace as we went through pre-set drills that were very familiar to the Japanese students, but very different from what we foreigners were accustomed to doing. I had been practicing Aikido for more than two decades, but I felt like a beginner and could do very little correctly. The drills, however, were an excellent way of developing harmonising, tai sabaki [18] and light and speedy footwork.

I didn't appreciate how helpful it actually was until I returned to Tokyo and resumed practice with a more familiar style of Aikido. Each morning in Kumamoto we got up at six am, swept the area around the dojo and temple free of leaves, and by 6.30 am we were on the mat ready for class.

We trained morning, afternoon and evening. The high point of the day was breakfast: unforgettable custard doughnuts at the local Mr Doughnut shop, washed down with cups of café au-lait. The

112

Japanese waitresses were polite and attentive and happily refilled our cups at no extra cost. In spite of that, during my short time in Japan – just less than three weeks – I lost seven kilos in weight.

The kokyu ryoku [19] exercises were particularly interesting and helped to develop a feeling of non-resistance that took relaxation to another level. Since most of my training had been in Ki Aikido, I was familiar with relaxation and Ki extension. But this was a different feeling. The emphasis in the Aiki Manseido style of Aikido taught in Kumamoto is to trust yourself entirely to the point of contact when your partner takes hold of you, without adding anything.

The 'unbendable arm' feeling emphasised so much in Ki Aikido actually becomes a hindrance to developing kokyu ryoku. It is felt as a 'locking up' of the body, which very quickly gets in the way. In Kokyu ryoku, when your partner lets go of your arm it should fall to your side quite naturally, as if a support had suddenly been withdrawn. In the style that I was used to, the arm is invariably left extended in space, supported by the muscles of the upper body.

Kokyu ryoku is very difficult to master. To do it successfully you have to overcome yourself and remove any desire to defeat or dominate your partner. When it works it is overwhelmingly powerful. According to the late Sunadomari Sensei, head of Aiki Manseido (he passed away in 2010) Kokyu ryoku is a spiritual discipline that serves to purify the heart.

He believed that we can come to practice Aikido in the way that O Sensei directed: as one with the loving power of the universe. But this is not something a teacher can give to his students. Each person must find it for themselves through diligent practice. When receiving this Kokyu ryoku feeling it is unmistakeable, yet very difficult to reproduce.

"From here forward, we must manifest the true spirit of Japanese culture. Furthermore, we must cease in pursuit of power based on the lower spirit, instead activating and giving rise to our higher spirit, and advancing forward based on the principle of non-resistance which neither competes nor collides with our partner. At any rate, this is the part that I am doing to help bring about harmony

in the world." (Attributed to Morihei Ueshiba in Enlightenment through Aikido, by Kanshu Sunadomari)

Towards the end of the Gasshuku, Sunadomari Sensei came to Kumamoto to conduct a Seminar. We foreigners were invited to meet him privately and he took the time to welcome us individually, scrutinising each of us closely.

During the seminar Sunadomari Sensei demonstrated some suwariwaza [20] techniques and, as is the tradition in Aiki Manseido, everyone was given the opportunity to feel his Kokyu ryoku. It was an amazing opportunity. And I couldn't help but contrast how different this was from what I was used to at home where teachers demonstrate with a few chosen ukes, and the bulk of students seldom get the opportunity to feel the teacher's technique.

When Sunadomari Sensei had finished demonstrating a technique, we would all do our best to practice what he had shown. His most senior students raced towards our little group of foreigners, and looked genuinely disappointed when others got there first.

After the seminar we went to the Aiki Manseido Hombu Dojo where we had snacks, green tea, and the ubiquitous sake served by dark suited boys and girls from the local university. I recognised some of them from the Shodo class they had given earlier in the week, an activity I enjoyed. As I recall, Hamada Sensei sat next to me. Not really the best spot, since as a non-drinker I quietly passed the generous cups of sake in his direction. He didn't seem to mind over much.

At one point Sunadomari Sensei started playing what sounded like old campaign tunes from a bygone age on a harmonica, with everyone singing along in time with the music. It was nostalgic and rousing at the same time.

Although unable to understand Japanese, I found myself strangely moved by this spirit of unabashed sentiment. I felt that I was witnessing a sensibility that is all too rare in our present post-postmodern era - a heartfelt expression of feeling, totally lacking in self-consciousness and devoid of complexity.

I wondered, too, if it would survive into the future. There was something innocent, simple and uncomplicated in this gathering of gentle people. It would change, I knew. They were a family, bound together around a kind and devoutly spiritual patriarch. I knew it wouldn't always be like this, but somehow I felt optimistic as I recalled the Founder's words:

"This budo will flourish from the country of fire".

The following day we travelled up into the high country, stopping off at a mountain Dojo where we practiced weapons 'Aiki Manseido' style for two hours. From there we carried on up to Mount Aso, Kumamoto's biggest and most active volcano. The surrounding countryside was like a scene from one of Kurosawa's epic films, with undulating hills swathed in tufted grasses that swayed rhythmically in the breeze.

Mount Aso itself was very active that day. The sulphur clouds were so thick that we could not stay too close to the mouth of the volcano for long; the acrid, cough inducing fumes brought tears to our eyes and we had to stay on the lee side of the crater for our own safety.

On the way back we stopped off at an 'onsen'[21] in the foothills of Mount Aso to bathe in geothermal spring water. On that day I fell in love with the country of fire. I had six days of intensive training, friendly and considerate company throughout and had seen some wonderful sights. I was content.

On my way back to Tokyo from Kumamoto, on the famous high speed Bullet Train (Shinkansen), I watched the countryside rushing by at hopeless speed. On one side I could see the mountains that run like a spine along the length of the Japanese islands, and on the other green fields butting up against factory complexes stretching out to the coast.

Outside it was a beautiful day and trees displayed an assortment of gold, amber and russet foliage. Off in the distance Mount Fuji floated majestically into view, a silent powerhouse of a mountain with an ancestral and regal demeanour. The sky was clear and the sun bright.

A few clouds paid court at the base of Fujiyama's snow-capped and ice bejewelled crown, glistening in the late morning sun. Tokyo was not far away. More training awaited me but I knew I would be doing less. My knees were badly swollen and I now only went into restaurants that had chairs.

In the end I was far from disappointed with my trip to Japan. At the time I did not realise how much I had learned. It was only later when I got back to my own dojo that I understood just how much I had been given, and how much study I still had to do. It was another beginning.

Human beings today, as in the remote past, have their being in the middle ground, between heaven and earth. This is an ancient motif running through many cultures, as much a part of our Anglo-Saxon and Celtic heritage as it is of the peoples of the Ural Altaic regions and South East Asia.

The Japanese people in recent times have astounded the world with the way they have coped with disasters on a massive scale. They have displayed a resilience of spirit and nobility of character that we cannot help but admire.

This inner strength is part of who we are as human beings. In the last analysis, it is the greatest renewable resource we have. If we share it with others it simply gets stronger. As beings standing between heaven and earth we are all potentially agents of power.

We have been like this for far longer than our modern, rational sensibilities would have us believe. Nature has bequeathed us from the outset with the capacity to bring mind and body together and build a bridge that leads to a more secure future:

"Aikido is the way of misogi (purification) itself, the way to become Sarutahiko-no-O-Kami (generative principle) and stand on the Ame-no-Ukihashi (the bridge between heaven and earth)."

Morihei Ueshiba.

That bridge is inside each one of us. By unifying mind and body, living each day in the present ('naka-ima') we can scale the tree of the world that unites heaven and earth. Ancient man knew this, and employed Shamans as 'spirit guides' to lead him in the right direction in times of difficulty.

Today we use psychotherapists as modern-day Shamans to bring us back from the abyss. The father of modern psychoanalysis, Sigmund

Freud, was well aware of the relationship between 'mythos' and 'logos' and noted how one passes into the other with time. His contemporary, Carl Jung, knew of the transformational capacity of the human spirit and knew that it would revolutionise psychology if it could be understood.

But regardless of terminology, archaic or scientific, the language employed by both expresses a truth that is universal about the immanent nature of the spirit. It exists inside each one of us. It is experienced as a sense of wholeness, peace and tranquillity. It is at the very root of our being in the most troubled of times, and present even when obscured by suffering.

To practice in the dojo is not just about learning techniques to throw someone down or immobilise them in a painful lock. In his book Aikido and Enlightenment Kanshu Sunadomari quotes from the Founder of Aikido:

"Aiki is love. It is the path that brings our hearts into oneness with the spirit of the universe to complete our mission in life by instilling in us a love and reverence for all of nature."

In my own limited experience, whether from Zen training or Aikido, the benefit of practice is a profound feeling of relaxation and expansiveness. It leads to a powerful sense of calmness and an alert clarity of mind. It is a feeling that arises naturally.

The 'Do' in Aikido denotes a path. The kanji character (道) represents a foot walking on that path. Through our connection with the earth we can unite with our higher nature and build a bridge between heaven and earth. This is the way of true power. It is our natural heritage as human beings.

Celtic Tree of Life (Crann Bethadh)

About the Author

This book is Alister Gillies' first, but he is an occasional blogger and contributor to online magazines. He has written a number of articles on a wide range of subjects ranging from bullying in the work place, to transplant tourism.

Alister's background is in project development. He is trained in counselling and personal development. He studied English Literature at the University of Glagow, and was the University's Alastair Buchan Poetry Prize Winner in 1987.

He has worked in a number of different sectors, some of which include social housing, justice, addiction, community development and teaching. He works with organisations, groups and individuals helping them to negotiate and manage effective change.

He has been writing for many years, and is a published poet. He also writes short stories, blogs and occasional articles about Aikido philosophy and practice. He is a Fourth Dan Aikido teacher and runs a dojo in Shrivenham, near Swindon. He likes to travel, and frequently goes to Europe to attend Aikido Seminars.

Notes

[1] Self-power or spiritual power

[2] DO = path or way. BU = the spear: 'the way of the spear'. But also BU = to stop: therefore 'the way to stop the spear'. The implication is in terms of yin and yang and Taoism – defence and offence are one and accord with the Tao.

[3] Misogi –Shinto ritual purification

[4] Japanese author of books and essays on Buddhism and Zen. He lectured at many Western universities.

[5] Diplomat, author and psychotherapist

[6] In 2002 Maraini was honoured by an award from the Japanese Photographic Society recognising his achievements and contribution to fine-art photography, the ethnology of the Ainu of Hokkaido and his efforts to strengthen ties between Japan and Italy spanning some sixty years

[7] Japanese martial artist and Founder of Japanese yoga (July 20, 1876–December 1, 1968)

[8] Literally "correct sitting"

[9] William Blake 1757 –1827, Auguries of Innocence

[10] Yamaoka Tesshu, 1836 –1888

[11] Special training

[12] Art of falling in Aikido

[13] In Japanese: one especially skilled in Aikido. It is used by others as an honorific but never used to describe oneself

[14] A partnered and seated exercise designed to develop breath power

[15] Moriteru Ueshiba, head of Aikikai organisation

[16] Aikikai HQ

[17] Training clothing

[18] Whole body movement

[19] Mind body coordination

[20] Seated techniques

[21] Hot springs used for public bathing

Chapter Illustrations

Ten Ox-herding (or "Ten Bulls") pictures, created by the 15th century Japanese Rinzai Zen monk Shubun. They are said to be copies of originals, now lost, traditionally attributed to Kakuan, a 12th century Chinese Zen Master.

CPSIA information can be obtained at www.ICGtesting.com
Printed in the USA
LVOW06s0210190815

450606LV00026B/525/P

9 781475 279825